# PRAYING
# PAUL'S LETTERS

# PRAYING
# PAUL'S LETTERS

BOOK SEVEN IN THE SERIES PRAYING THE SCRIPTURES

Elmer L. Towns

# Praying Paul's Letters

Romans

1 Corinthians

2 Corinthians

Galatians

Ephesians

Philippians

Colossians

1 Thessalonians

2 Thessalonians

1 Timothy

2 Timothy

Titus

Philemon

DESTINY IMAGE® PUBLISHERS, INC.

P.O. Box 310, Shippensburg, PA 17257-0310

*"Speaking to the Purposes of God for this Generation and for the Generations to Come."*

This book and all other Destiny Image, Revival Press, Mercy Place, Fresh Bread, Destiny Image Fiction, and Treasure House books are available at Christian bookstores and distributors worldwide.

ISBN-13: 978-0-7394-9610-7

For Worldwide Distribution, Printed in the U.S.A.

# TABLE OF CONTENTS

## COLOSSIANS

## 1 THESSALONIANS

## 2 THESSALONIANS

## 1 TIMOTHY

## 2 TIMOTHY

## TITUS

## PHILEMON

# PRAYING WITH ME
# THE LETTERS OF PAUL

This project began four years ago when one morning I began translating Psalm 37 into popular everyday English, then transposing it into the second person—a prayer to God. Psalm 37 went well, so I translated Psalm 34. Then I decided to translate the whole book of Psalms, not for a book for other people, but for my own spiritual growth. I wanted to pray the Psalms.

When I mentioned the project to Don Milam, editor at Destiny Image Publishing, he said, "I want to publish that book." And so in 2004, I released *Praying the Psalms*. Since that time, five other books have been released in the series *Praying the Scriptures*.

Now I invite you to join me in *Praying Paul's Letters*. If you do more than read the words of Paul—if you pray them from your heart—they will transform your life. The Bible does that.

*Praying* the Scriptures is superior to *reading* the Scriptures, because normal reading of the Bible deals with the intellect—you pass the message through your mind. But when you *Pray the Scriptures*, you go to a deeper level—to the heart. Your emotions become involved in the message, and then you move your will; for when you talk to God through the Scriptures, you have chosen to worship God and obey Him. *Praying Paul's Letters* will touch your intellect, emotion, and will. That's how your life will be transformed.

Rather than including dictionary facts as an introduction to each of Paul's letters, I have written a story to incorporate the facts about Paul's writings—where he was when he was writing a particular letter, why he wrote, what he wanted to say, and what he wanted to accomplish in the lives of those who received his letters. The stories are the way I think it happened, including the way I think Paul felt when he wrote each letter. Obviously the stories are not inspired. But basic facts are included to help give you insight into each letter and help you apply it to your life.

As you are *Praying Paul's Letters*, may you touch God in a new way—but in a greater way, may God touch you.

Sincerely yours in Christ,
Elmer L. Towns
Written at my home at the foot of
the Blue Ridge Mountains

# Romans

## THE STORY OF WRITING
## THE BOOK OF ROMANS

Date: A.D. 60 ⌒ Written in: Corinth, Greece ⌒ Written by: Paul

I was sitting with several of my followers in a home in Corinth. The room was stuffy, but we were out of the sun. We were watching the long shadows of the afternoon darken the house.

I told the group that I had a great desire to preach the Gospel in Rome. I told them when we preach in Rome, we are reaching the world. I reminded them all the roads of the world lead to Rome, which means we can use them to travel the opposite way into all the world.

One of my followers said, "Paul, you can't go to Rome, the city is too big, sin is too rampant. The city is given to idolatry because Caesar Augustus recently built or restored 82 temples. Don't forget the politics; the Senate has just built a new forum. The city is given over to the sins of the flesh and to pleasure. The new coliseum has free admission for chariot races, gladiatorial contests, and theatrical performances. They would like nothing more than to throw you to the lions in the middle of that massive arena."

The rest of the followers said nothing, but their eyes darted from one to another to see the reaction of the others. Then they all looked at me, I was their leader. I had never backed down from a challenge, and I never went to a city that I did not evangelize.

The room was silent, an ordinary house fly, oblivious to imminent eternal decision, buzzed around the room. The only other thing heard was the deep breaths of some of the followers.

I did not say anything, but rose slowly, walked to an open window and looked down the street of Corinth. "There was not one Christian when I came to this town; Corinth was known as the most sinful harbor town on the Mediterranean Sea."

I looked around the room, then pointed down the street, "There is the place where I made tents for Aquila and Pricilla, and over there"—pointing across the street—"is where they lived. It was around their evening meal when they came to believe in Jesus Christ as their personal Messiah. From them the Gospel spread to the synagogue and many Jews believed."

I walked to the other side of the room and pushed open a door. Immediately, the evening breeze stirred the room. From the door we could see the Aegean Sea. Again I pointed, "There is the synagogue and next to it is the home of Justice. Remember, we led all the Christians out of the synagogue, and they began holding church service in Justice House. I want all my followers to remember what God did in Corinth."

I looked around the room. "This was one of the most wicked cities in Greece, yet the Gospel captured the hearts of many. Yes, and Rome is just as wicked and I am committed to preaching the Gospel in every wicked place where Christ is not known."

I moved around the room vigorously returning to the door that overlooked the sea and pointing out to the railway. "There is the railway where boats are put on railcars and pulled over the isthmus. They do that to save five or six sailing days to Rome. Every hour a boat is pulled over the narrow strip of ground, and every hour a ship leaves—taking the Gospel with them."

I reminded them that many Christians worked on the railway pulling railcars over that small strip of land. While sailors were waiting for the boats to be pulled over, they visited taverns and houses of prostitution. But Christians met their ship, and witnessed to them that Jesus the Messiah died for their sins. Many times when a ship sailed from Corinth they had Christians on board who would carry the Gospel to ports throughout the Mediterranean Sea.

Then I told them, "Where one ship may leave the harbor of Corinth every hour, there could be thousands of people leaving Rome every day on the Appian Way, going around the world with the Gospel."

That was the end of the conversation. Before the men left, I told Tertius I had a job for him. I asked him to meet me early the next morning.

The next morning I rose early and met Tertius on the back patio of the home. I explained to him that in the coming weeks I would be writing the most important letter of my life to the people in Rome. Because Rome was the center of the world, I felt they needed a letter that explained Christianity from beginning to end, from Alpha to Omega.

I laid out my project, then said to Tertius, "Get ink, pen, and paper, for you must write this epistle for me. My eyes are too weak to do it—but I will read carefully every word that you write and sign it with my signature." I explained that the letter needed authority, it needed my signature as an apostle of grace.

I could read, but not very clearly and not very fast. Sometimes it took a little while for the letters on the page to form in my mind. Ever since I had been stoned in Lystra, I had problems with my eyes. I've often thought that a stone probably damaged a nerve or maybe even a sharp stone punctured the retina.

In the early days I had written every word of my letters with my own hands. I had written to the Galatians—my first letter—"See how I have written such large letters."

But this letter to the Romans would be much longer, and if I used giant block letters, it would probably take several large scrolls. I wanted this letter to be on one scroll, because I knew it would be copied by the church in Rome and sent to all other churches. Also, itinerate preachers coming through Rome would make a copy to take this letter to other outlying churches. This letter would be circulated throughout the Mediterranean world. If there were two or three scrolls, one may be lost, and then people would not have a complete copy of God's magnificent plan of salvation.

Tertius returned with the writing box, took a scroll and unrolled it. Tertius had made a new batch of ink for this special project. He crushed the black coals from the fire into powder, and then mixed it with olive oil. Tertius stirred the mixture into ink, then inserted the quill in the ink, pressed the barrel of the feather so that it would drink up ink, and he was ready to write. Tertius ask, "What will be the first word?"

I smiled, then spoke slowly, "Paul, a bondservant of Jesus Christ, called to be an apostle, separated to the Gospel of God which the Father promised through His prophets." Nothing could be heard on the back patio except the scratching of the quill on the parchment.

Sincerely yours in Christ,
The apostle Paul

---

Sitting there on the patio in Corinth, the two men wrote the greatest explanation of the Gospel ever penned by humans. Why the greatest? Because Paul was inspired by the Holy Spirit to write accurately what God wanted Him to write.

# PRAYING THE BOOK OF ROMANS

## Introduction and the Guilt of the Heathen

### Romans 1:1-32

Lord, the apostle Paul wrote to the Christians in Rome telling them he was a
servant who was chosen to preach the Good News,
which You promised in the Old Testament through the prophets.

*May I always be faithful to my calling,*
*As Paul was to his task.*

Lord, thank You for the Gospel about Your Son, the Lord Jesus Christ.
Who came as a baby though King David's line, who was raised
from the dead by the Spirit of Holiness to demonstrate that He
was the mighty Son of God.

Lord, thank You that through Christ all your mercy has been poured out
on me to be a witness to everyone, everywhere about Your grace;
so they too can believe and become a Christ follower.

Lord, Paul told his dear friends in Rome that You loved them and called them;
Paul prayed for grace and peace to rest on them from You—God the
Father—and from the Lord Jesus Christ.

*May Your grace and peace fill my life,*
*As I walk in Your love and calling.*

Lord, Paul told everyone about the faith of the Roman believers, and
that it was
his duty to serve You by continually praying for them.
Paul specifically prayed that he would have the opportunity to

have a safe trip to come see them. He wanted to strengthen their spiritual gifts so their church would grow strong spiritually.

Lord, Paul wanted to bless the Roman church by sharing his faith with them, and allow them to be a blessing to him.

Lord, Paul told the Romans that he planned many times before to visit them, but was prevented. He wanted to minister to them just as he had ministered in other Gentile churches.

Lord, I have a debt to carry the Gospel to both civilized people, and to unreached people groups who have never heard the Gospel.

Lord, I am ready to preach to any or to all, just as Paul was ready to preach the Gospel to those in Rome and to everyone in the world.

Lord, I am not ashamed of the Good News of Christ, for it is powerful to get people to believe so they can be saved.

Lord, I agree with the priority that Paul gave, that the Gospel must first be preached to the Jews, then to Gentiles. When a person puts his personal trust in the Gospel, You declare them righteous—fit for Heaven. This is what the Old Testament teaches, "The just shall live by expressing faith."

## Why the Heathen Are Lost

### Romans 1:18-32

Lord, You have revealed that You will punish everyone who trespasses Your commandments because they reject the truth given them. You have revealed Yourself to everyone's conscience. Also, everyone can plainly learn from nature that it took a powerful Creator to create this vast universe, and that it took an intelligent Creator to put the laws of nature in place to control everything.

Lord, now no one can give an excuse when they are judged and
condemned because everyone knows You exist and You have
eternal power.

Lord, everyone knows You exist, but they won't acknowledge You, or
thank You for natural blessings, or even worship You. They are
controlled by illogical thought patterns because they reject the
logic of Your existence.
Their minds are blinded and confused. When they think they are
wise, they actually are foolish. Instead of worshiping Your
glorious presence, they worship gods made out of wood, or
stone that look like birds, or animals, or snakes, or corrupt people.

Lord, You allowed those who reject You to do all types of sexual sins, so
that they can fulfill their lust, degrading their bodies with one
another. Instead of believing the truth they knew about You, they
deliberately rejected You, choosing to worship and serve created
idols rather than You, the Creator, who could bless them.

Lord, You abandoned them to their passions because their woman
turned from natural sexual practices to abnormal acts. Their men
turned from normal relations with women and turned to lustful
sexual practices with one another, men behaving indecently with
men, so that they pay a penalty with their souls for their perversion.

Lord, since they refused to acknowledge You—You gave them up to
their own irrational and corrupt ideas. Now they continually try
to think up new and sexually stimulating ideas that the depraved
mind conceives. They are controlled by all sorts of evil and greed,
and hatred, and fightings, bitterness, and lies; so that they even
want to kill those who mistreat them. They quarrel, hate You, are
proud, braggardly and continually think of new ways to sin, and
hate their parents. They don't understand what is right, nor do
they know how to do right. They break their promises, are mean
and have no feelings for others. They know in their hearts You

will judge them, but they deny it outwardly. They go ahead and
do all these things in rebellion against You, and seek friendship
with others who also against You.

Lord, I know that You alone are God and that sin
  is denial of Your existence and rejection of Your Laws.

*Give me faith to always trust You,*
  *And give me courage to always follow Your plan of living.*

Amen.

## The Guilt of Religious People

### Romans 2:1-29

Lord, people have no excuse for their personal sin,
  Because they criticize others who do the same sin.
In judging others, they condemn themselves
  Because they behave no differently than those they condemn.

Lord, You condemn all who rebel against Your Laws,
  And you punish law-breakers impartially.
Those who pass judgment on other people
  Will be judged because they do the exact same things.

Lord, You are patient with those who sin against You,
  You wait a long time before punishing them.
You are giving them an opportunity to repent
  And turn to You from their sins;
  Your goodness should lead them to repentance.

But no, their stubborn refusal only adds
  To Your anger toward them.
Then one day they will suffer punishment
  When You punish everyone for their sins

Just as the Scriptures teach,
  "God will repay each as their works deserve."

Lord, those who seek Your honor and immortality
  Will earn eternal life from You.
Those who refuse Your truth and do evil,
  You will punish in Your anger and fury.
They will suffer pain and suffering
  Because they rebelled against You and chased evil,
  This includes both Jews and Gentiles as well.
But, there will be glory, honor, and peace,
  To those who seek Your salvation,
  Including both Jews and Gentiles as well.

Lord, there is no favoritism of persons with You,
  You will punish Gentiles when they sin
  Even if they never heard of Your written Law.
You will punish those who have access to Your Law,
  They will be judged by what's in the Law.

But I realize it is not knowing the Law,
  But, keeping the Law that makes anyone holy.
Gentiles who have never heard the Law
  Know by their conscience what the Law requires.
They know by their reason to obey the Law,
  Even when they don't "possess" copies of the Law.
The substance of the Law is written in their hearts,
  They know right from wrong.
Their conscience accuses them when they sin,
  Or it excuses them when they do right.

Lord, You will punish the Jews when they sin,
  Because they disobey the written Law that they possess;
  They know what is right, but don't do it.

No one is saved because they know what is right,
    They are saved when they do it.

Lord, the day is coming when Jesus Christ
    Will judge the secrets of all people.
I will be ready to meet You in judgment
    For I have been saved and I live for You.

Lord, those who called themselves Jews
    Should walk according to the Law of God,
    And honor You with their lives.
The Jews should know Your will because they know Your Law,
    And they should know what is right and wrong.
The Jews should be guides to the blind,
    And they should be a beacon to those in the dark.
They should teach the ignorant and unlearned,
    Because they embody all knowledge and truth.
But the Jews do not live by the Law,
    They should teach themselves what they teach others.
They preach against stealing, yet they steal;
    They forbid adultery, yet they commit adultery.
They despise idols, yet they make money off idol making;
    They boast about the Law, yet they break it
    And thereby dishonor You who gave the Law.
As the Scriptures teach, "It is your fault, Jews,
    That God's name is despised by the Gentiles."

        Amen.

## All Are Lost in Sin

## Romans 3:1-31

Lord, Paul asked if there is an advantage of being Jewish,
    Does circumcision mean any thing?

Paul answers "Yes, being a Jew has many advantages,
    They received Your message in the Old Testament.
Yet, even when some Jews were unfaithful,
    Their lack of faith didn't cancel Your promises.
God, You will always keep Your Word
    Even when everyone else is unfaithful.
The Book of Psalms says, "The Word of God,
    Will always prove to be right,
    No matter who questions God."
Some point out that the sins of the Jews
    Make You demonstrate Your holiness,
    Because You always judge sin.
The Jews justify their sin
    Claiming people will say, You—God—are good
    When they see You punishing our sin.
Then the Jews ask, "Is it fair for You to punish us
    When our sin helps others recognize You?"
Paul answers, "That is absurd thinking,
    It means God could never judge sin
    If God didn't judge rebellious Jews."
Paul continues, "That's like saying my lying
    Makes You demonstrate Your truthfulness."
"When You judge the Jews' sin,
    You thus bring glory to Yourself."
That's like saying, "We do evil
    To bring about good."

Lord, Paul asked again, "Are Jews better off than Gentiles?"
    He answers, "No, both are under sin's control."
The Scriptures teach
    There is no good person left in the world,
    No not one.
There is no one who understands You
    And no one is seeking You.

All have turned from doing right,
>    There is no good person on earth, no not one.
Their speech is rebellious and filthy,
>    Just like an open grave.
Their tongue is full of deceit,
>    Bitter curses fill their mouth, and
>    Their words are deadly like a snake's poison.
They are quick to stab people in the back,
>    Creating misery and strife wherever they go.
They know nothing of Your blessing
>    And they don't care what You think of them.

Lord, the Jews should know what the Law says,
>    And they are responsible to obey what You say.
Therefore the Jews stand guilty before You
>    When they see clearly they aren't obeying You,
>    So they know they are sinners.

Lord, You have spoken to silence every mouth,
>    Now the whole world is guilty before You.
Therefore, no one can be justified
>    By keeping the Law;
>    Rather the Law makes us conscious of our sin.

Lord, I thank You that Your righteousness is made known
>    Apart from knowing the Law,
>    It is made known through the Gospel.
Now there is a way to Heaven for all sinners,
>    You will declare us "not guilty"
>    When we trust Christ for salvation.
>    All can be saved—Jews and Gentiles—alike,
>    By believing in Jesus Christ.

Lord, I know I am a sinner, because You said
>    All have sinned,

And come short of Your glorious benefits.
But both Jew and Gentile are declared righteous
 Through Your free gift of grace
 When they are redeemed by Jesus Christ.

Lord, you sent Jesus to take the punishment for our sins,
 And reconciled us to You.
You declared that sins committed before the Cross
 Are forgiven by the blood of Christ
And declared that all sins committed,
 At this time are forgiven.
In this way You make Your righteousness known;
 Therefore, Your wrath against sin is justified,
 And You become the Justifier for sinners.

Lord, I realize I can't boast about anything
 That has to do with my salvation,
Because my forgiveness is not based on what I do,
 But is based on what Christ has done for me.

Therefore, all Christians are justified by faith
 Without keeping the Law.
You are not saving only Jews—no,
 You treat everyone the same way,
 Whether they are Jew or Gentile.
This does not undermine the Law—no!
 When we realize salvation is by faith alone,
 This places the Law in its proper place.
    Amen.

## Justification by Faith

### Romans 4:1-25

Lord, Paul points out Abraham is the founder
    From which all Jews descended.
If Abraham were justified by doing something good,
    He would have had something to boast about.
But the Scriptures teach, "Abraham believed God,
    And God declared him as righteous."
When someone works, they get wages;
    They get what's due to them.
However, when a man gets salvation free,
    He has not worked for it;
You have justified him because of faith.

Lord, David said the same thing,
    "A man is happy when he is forgiven
    Without doing good works."
That man is blessed because his sins
    Are no longer written in Your book.
Is this a blessedness only for the circumcised Jews?
    Or can Gentiles be justified before You?
Look again at Abraham, he was justified
    By You before he was circumcised.
When Abraham was later circumcised,
    It was an outer sign of faith within his heart.
In this way, Abraham became the spiritual father
    Of all the uncircumcised believers
    So they might also be justified by God.
Your promise to Abraham that he would be
    The spiritual father to all believers, of all times,
    Was based on his faith, not his works.
If unsaved people can receive Your forgiveness

By keeping the Law,
　　Then our faith is pointless and empty.
The Law teaches we are punished for breaking the Law
　　But Christ has fulfilled the Law in His death;
　　He has taken it out of the way.
So, we get Your blessings by faith,
　　Whether we keep the Law or not.
You will bless those who belong to the Law
　　As well as Gentiles who weren't given the Law,
　　As long as we all come to You by faith.
We come like Abraham, who is the father of us all;
　　The Scriptures promise, "I have made Abraham
　　The ancestor of many nations."
God called those things that are not, i.e.,
　　The salvation of the Gentiles
　　As though it had already happened.

Lord, when You told Abraham he would have a son,
　　And be the father of many nations,
Abraham believed Your promises to him;
　　He hoped against any hope of his present circumstances.
Abraham did not have weak faith
　　Even though his body couldn't reproduce
　　And he was 100 years old.
Also, Abraham realized Sarah was barren and old, but
　　He staggered not at Your promises through unbelief,
　　But was strong in faith giving glory to You.
Abraham was convinced You had all power
　　To do what You promised.
Because of Abraham's faith, You forgave his sins,
　　And declared him righteous.

Lord, I know this kind of faith wasn't for Abraham alone,
　　But it is for me also;

You will accept me as You accepted Abraham.
I too believe Your promises
That just as You brought Jesus back from the dead,
You will forgive all my sins
And declare me righteous before You.
Amen.

## The Results of Justification by Faith

### Romans 5:1-21

Lord, now that I'm declared right with You by faith,
I can experience lasting peace.
Since my faith in Jesus, I can enter Your grace,
I can boast of looking forward to Your glory.
Also, I can rejoice in my sufferings,
Knowing they work patience in my life.
And patience produces endurance and when I endure,
I get Your approval which gives me hope.
My hope does not disappoint me, because You
Have poured Your love into my heart
By the Holy Spirit whom You gave me.

Lord, at the moment when I was helpless,
I realized Christ died for sinful people, such as me.
I wouldn't expect anyone to die for a good person,
Even though that is possible,
But You demonstrated Your great love for me
By sending Christ to die for me,
While I was a great sinner.
Since His blood has done all this for me,
He will also declare me completely righteous.

Lord, when Jesus' death reconciled me to You,
     I was still not saved,
     I was still Your enemy.
Now that I am reconciled
     Surely I can count on Your blessings
     By the life of Your Son living in me.
I rejoice in this wonderful new relationship
     With the Lord Jesus Christ
     Based on what He did in saving me.

Lord, I know when Adam sinned, sin entered the world
     Then all people sinned
     And death spread throughout the human race.
Sin existed in the world
     Long before the written Law was given.
No one could be accused of breaking the Law,
     When there was no written Law.
Yet, all people died from Adam to Moses;
     It was their sin that led to their death,
     It was not a matter of their breaking the written Law.

Lord, Adam was a contrast to Christ,
     So the gift of Christ outweighed the fall of Adam.
Through one man—Adam—many died,
     Through the gift of one man—Christ— many lived.
The results of the gift of Christ
     Outweigh the results of Adam's fall.
For after the Fall came the judgment of condemnation,
     And many committed trespasses because of the Fall,
     But by the one Man—Jesus Christ—came abundant life.
For it is certain that death reigned
     Over everyone because of one man's fall.
It is even more certain that life reigns
     Because of one man—Jesus Christ—who gives

The free gift to those who don't deserve it.
Again, Adam's sin brought punishment on all,
But Christ made it possible for all to be declared righteous.
By one man's disobedience, many were made sinners;
By one man's obedience, many will be declared righteous.

Lord, the Law was given to show all
How far short they come in obeying You.
The more we see our sins and failures,
The more we realize how much You have forgiven us.
Before, sin reigned over all, bringing death;
Now grace reigns to deliver eternal life
To those who are in Christ Jesus our Lord.
Amen.


## Deliverance From Sin in the Believer's Life

### Romans 6:1-23

Lord, should I keep sinning
So you can keep showing Your grace?
Absolutely not!
Sin's power over me is broken;
Should I keep sinning
When I don't have to? Again, no!
When I was placed into Christ by Spiritual baptism,
I was placed into His death;
The control of my sin nature over me
was broken by His death.
In other words, when I was baptized into Christ,
I died when He died.
When Christ was raised up from the dead,
I was given new life to live for Him.

Lord, I have been united with Christ in death.
      That I might share His new life.
My old lustful nature was nailed to the Cross,
      It received a death-blow
        So that I might not serve sin in the future.
For when I am dead to sin,
      I am free from all its power over me.
I believe that having died with Christ,
      I now share my new life with Him.

Lord, since Christ has been raised from the dead,
      He will never again die;
      Death has no power over Him.
Christ died once for all to end sin's control,
      Now He lives in Heaven with You.
So, I look on myself as dead to sin's control,
      But alive to Your will through Jesus Christ.
I will not let sin control my physical body
      And I will not obey its sinful lust.
I will not let any part of my body
      Become an evil tool to be used for sinning.
I give myself to you as one who is alive from the dead,
      And I give all parts of my body to you,
      As an instrument of righteousness.
I will not let sin control me,
      I will not be controlled by the Law, but by grace.

Lord, shall I continue to sin because
      I am not under the law?
      Absolutely not!
If I give myself to sin,
      I become a slave to the one I obey.
I cannot be a slave to sin and death,
      And at the same time be a slave to Christ and life.

Lord, thank You that I'm no longer a slave to sin,
    But I'm your slave,
    Having believed Your principles from my heart.
I am free from the mastery of my old nature
    And I am a slave to righteousness.

Lord, once I was a slave to uncleanliness and self-gratification,
    Now I am a slave to righteousness and holiness.
When I was a slave to sin,
    I felt no obligation to obey Your will.
I got nothing from serving sin,
    And now I am ashamed of what I did,
    Because those things lead to death.
But now I have been set free from sin,
    I have become Your slave
    That will lead to holiness and eternal life.
When I serve sin, I earn the wages of death,
    But You gave me eternal life through Christ Jesus, my Lord.
                Amen.

## The Struggle of the Old and New Nature

### Romans 7:1-25

Lord, Paul told his saved Jewish brethren
    When they died to the Law,
    It no longer held them in its power.
A married woman has legal obligations
    To the husband while he is alive.
All obligations came to an end,
    When the husband dies.
But if she gives herself to another man,
    While her husband is still alive,
    She is legally an adulteress.

Nevertheless, her legal obligations cease
>When her husband dies,
>And she can legally marry another.

Lord, Paul said that is why Christians
>Who died to the Law in Christ's death,
Can now give themselves to Christ
>Who arose from the dead
>That they might bring fruit to You.
But when they give themselves to their sinful nature,
>Their lustful passions controlled their bodies
>So they bear fruit to death.
But now when we die to our lust that once controlled us,
>We are released from the Law
So we can serve You in a new way,
>Not by legalistically obeying rules and traditions
>But by the power of new life.

Lord, Paul told them the Law was not evil,
>Except that no one would have known what sin is
>Except that the Law told them.
I would have not known that "coveting" was evil,
>Except the Law said, "Thou shalt not covet."
The Law stirred up my evil desires
>By reminding me these desires were wrong.
Does that mean if there were no laws to break,
>There would be no sinning? No!
I felt OK as long as I was ignorant of the Law,
>But when I learned what the Law meant,
>I realized I was a sinner, I learned I was a slave doomed to die.
The Law was supposed to lead me to life,
>But instead it led me to death.
Sin took advantage of me by using the Law
>To give me a death sentence.

Lord, I know the Law is holy,
      And the Ten Commands are good and just.
Does that mean that something that was good
      Was responsible for my death?
      Absolutely not!
But sin is treacherous and deceitful,
      It used something good for evil purposes,
      Thus sin exercised all its lustful powers over me.

Lord, I know the Law is spiritual
      But I am unspiritual, sold as a slave to sin.
I cannot understand my reaction to things;
      What I am supposed to do,
      I don't do.
What I hate to do,
      I continually go back to do it.
When I act against what I want to do,
      That means the Law is good.
When I rebel against the Law,
      It is not me that's doing it,
      But sin that dwells in me.
I know that nothing good lives in me,
      It's my sinful nature that controls my life.
I have a desire to do good things, but
      I cannot carry it out.
When I try not to do wrong things,
      I do them anyway.
So when I do the things I don't want to do,
      Then it is not my true self doing them;
      Sin still controls my life.

Lord, I've discovered a new law in me,
      Every time I want to do good,
      I do wrong, intentionally.

I love to keep the Law of God,
> But I see another law working in me.

It fights the logic of my mind,
> Making me a prisoner of the Law,
> Working in my body to make me sin, it's my old nature.

What a miserable person I am.
> Who can rescue me from my slavery to sin?

Thank You, Lord, that You will deliver me
> Through Jesus Christ my Lord.

Lord, what is the result of all of this?
> In my lower nature I am a slave of sin,
> But in my mind I am Your slave.
>> Amen.

## The Power of the Holy Spirit in the Believer

### Romans 8:1-39

Lord, now there is no condemnation against me,
> Because I am in Christ Jesus.

The power of the life-giving Holy Spirit
> Is mine through Christ Jesus.

He has released me from the compulsive cycle
> Of sin and lust of my old nature.

For the Law was powerless to help me obey,
> Because I was a slave to my old nature.

But You sent Your Son in a human body
> To be a sacrificial offering for my sin
> To destroy sin's domination over me.

Now I can obey Your laws
> By following the leading of the Holy Spirit,
> And refusing the lust of my old nature.

Lord, those who are dominated by their sinful nature
      Have made up their minds to sin,
But I am dominated by the Holy Spirit,
      Because I have made up my mind
      To do what He desires of me.
If I follow the dictates of my old nature,
      It will lead to death.
When I obey the Holy Spirit,
      He leads me to life and peace.
As a result, when I only obey my old nature,
      I have made myself Your enemy.
My old nature has never been Your friend,
      And I can never make it obey You.
Those who only please their old nature,
      Never please You.

Lord, I am not interested in pleasing the old nature,
      I am interested in spiritual things,
      Because the Holy Spirit lives in my life.
And I know I am Your child,
      Because I possess the Holy Spirit.

Lord, even when my body is dead because of sin,
      My spirit is alive because I was declared righteous,
And the Holy Spirit who raised Jesus from the dead
      Lives in me to give me life.
Therefore, after this body is dead,
      I will live again by the same Holy Spirit
      Who is living within me.

Lord, I know it is not necessary for me
      To obey the lust of my old nature.
If I died physically obeying my old nature,
      I'd be doomed to death.
But Your Holy Spirit can stop my rebellion,

By His power that indwells me.
Therefore, I will be led by the Spirit of God,
    I will be Your child.

Lord, I am not just a slave who cowers in fear
    Of breaking laws or displeasing You,
But I received the Holy Spirit, who made me Your child,
    So I cry to you, "Papa, Father."
The Holy Spirit constantly tells my spirit
    That I am Your child;
Now if I am Your child, I am also an heir,
    Your heir, and co-heir with Christ.
Because I suffer as a Christian,
    I will also share in His glory in Heaven.

Lord, my present sufferings are nothing
    When compared with the glories
    That are waiting for me in Heaven.
As a matter of fact, all Creation groans,
    Waiting for the glorification of Your children
Because Creation will lose its thorns, thistles,
    And the curse you put upon it
    When You send Jesus at the end of time.
Creation will be liberated from its corruption
    To enjoy the same magnificent redemption
    You will give to all of Your children.
From the beginning until now, animals and plants groan,
    Expecting to be redeemed from the bondage of decadence
    To enjoy the same redemption as Your children.
I too groan while I wait for my body to be transformed,
    For that is my inward hope.
By trusting You, I'm looking forward to getting a new body;
    Those who are already in Heaven don't need hope
    They have already received their reward.

I continue to trust for something I don't have yet,
> But I wait patiently and confidently for it.

Lord, thank You for the help of the Holy Spirit
> Who comes to assist me in my weakness.
I don't know how I ought to pray
> But the Holy Spirit intercedes for me,
> He prays with words I can't understand or express.
What the Holy Spirit prays for me
> Is in agreement with You, my Heavenly Father.
Therefore, the things that will happen to me
> Are for my good because He prays for me.
For when You foreknew me, You predestinated me
> To be confirmed to the image of Your Son,
> So Your Son will be the first born among many children.

Lord, You predestined me and called me,
> Because You called me, You also justified me,
> And those You justified, You will glorify.

Lord, how shall I respond to Your great plan?
> If You are for me, who can be against me?
Since You did not hold back Your only Son,
> But You gave Him for us all,
> I know You will freely give me all things.
Who can bring any charge against Your children?
> Since You justify me, who can condemn me?
Christ Jesus who died for me and was raised,
> Stands at Your right hand to intercede for me.
Who can separate me from Your love?
> Not trouble, hardship, or persecutors,
> Hunger, nakedness, or danger.
The Scriptures teach, "I must be ready
> To die at any time, I am like sheep
> Awaiting slaughter."

These are all trials over which I must triumph
By the power of Christ who loves me,
And died for me.

Lord, I am positive nothing can separate me
From Your love for me.
Death can't separate me from You, also
Angels can't to it;
Neither can the satanic power of hell,
Nor things present, or things to come.

Nothing can separate me from Your love,
Not height, nor depth, nor any other creature,
For I am safe in Christ Jesus my Lord.
Amen.

## Continuing Jewish Unbelief

### Romans 9:1-33

Lord, Paul's conscience made him tell everyone that he had a deep desire that his Jewish relatives might be saved. He was willing to be cut off from Christ for their salvation. Paul had deep sorrow and mental anguish because the Jewish people rejected Christ.

*Lord, give me a burden for the salvation of my lost relatives and friends, that Paul had for the Jews who represented his flesh and blood.*

Lord, the Jewish people were adopted by You, and given Your covenants, and Your glory visited them. You gave them the Law and principles how to worship You. They had everything, but rejected You.

Lord, the Jewish people descended from the patriarch's and Christ came from their flesh and blood. Christ is the One whom they should worship above all, He is the One they should bless.

Lord, does this mean You have failed to keep your promises because the
Jews refused to recognize Christ? Absolutely not! Not all physical
Jews are spiritual Jews, and not all the physical descendants of
Abraham have the faith of Abraham. You promised that through
Isaac the spiritual promises would be carried out, which means
other physical children of Abraham didn't get the privilege of being
in the line of Christ. That means not all the physical children of
Abraham are his spiritual descendents, only those who are the
children of promise.

Lord, I believe Your promises to Abraham apply to me,
I have acted on the promises You made.
I recognized Jesus is the Messiah, the Son of God,
I have received Him by faith and I am saved.

Lord, Paul quoted your promise, "I will visit you and Sarah will have a son."
Then later you promised to Rebecca when she was pregnant by
Isaac, before her twin sons were born, and before either of them did
good or evil, that "The elder shall serve the younger." You chose
Jacob before he was born—because your choice is free—and it didn't
depend on human merit. The Scripture said, "Jacob I love, because
he is the child of promise." Does this make You unjust? No!
Remember what You said to Moses, "I will have mercy on whom I will
have mercy, and I will have compassion on whom I please."

Lord, I know the only thing that counts is Your mercy, not what people
desire or try to do. I am saved by Your grace.

Lord, thank You for having mercy on me.
I didn't deserve salvation and eternal life,
But you saved me by Your grace,
And made me a member of Your family.

Lord, You said to Pharaoh, "For this purpose I raised you up, so I might
show my great power and that my name may be known throughout

the world." Therefore, God shows mercy when He wants to show mercy, and He hardens those He wants to harden.

*Lord, thank You for sending the Holy Spirit*
*    To soften my heart to spiritual things.*
*Thank You for opening my blind eyes,*
*    And giving me a desire to know You.*

Lord, many will ask, "How can You ever punish anyone since no one can reject Your will?" Therefore You answer them, "What right has any human to question Me?" You created everyone. "The pot has no right to question the potter, 'Why have you made me this shape?'" Every potter—or craftsman—can do what he wills with the clay. He decides whether a lump of clay should be used for an extraordinary pot or an average pot.

*Lord, I thank You for making me who I am,*
*    And thank You for my special gifts.*
*Help me glorify You through my unique calling,*
*    And help me fulfill Your purpose for my life.*

Lord, You have a perfect right to show Your anger, at any time against those who rebel against You, even when You were originally patient with them. You put up with rebels so you can show Your mercy and richness of grace.

Lord, You are patient with us—both Jews and Gentiles—to reveal Your grace and kindness to us. You said in Scripture, "I will say to a people who are not my people, that you will be Mine. You are my people, I will say to a nation that I have not loved, I love you." They will be called the sons of the Living God.

Lord, You said "Though Israel should have as many descendants as there are grains of sand on the seashore, only a remnant will be saved. For You will swiftly carry out Your punishment once and for all. For the Scriptures said 'Unless You—the all-powerful Lord—show Your mercy, all Jews would be destroyed, just as You destroyed Sodom and Gomorrah.'"

Lord, then the Gentiles who were not looking for Your righteousness found it, they found Your righteousness that came by faith. The Jews who were trying to find Your righteousness by keeping the Law did not keep the Law and did not find righteousness. Why? Because they relied on their legalism, and not on faith. In other words, they stumbled over the Law and it became a stumbling stone to them. The Scriptures say, "You lay in Zion a stumbling stone—a rock to trip people up—that Rock was Jesus Christ. Those who believe in Him will not stumble or fall."

Amen.

## Salvation Is for Everyone

## Romans 10:1-21

Lord, Paul told the Romans that the longing of his heart was for Jewish people to be saved. Paul knows the enthusiasm they have for You, but it is misdirected zeal. Their passion is based on wrong knowledge. They have never realized Your demands of them for perfect righteousness, all the while they were trying to keep the Law to demonstrate their own righteousness. Therefore, all Jews, along with all Gentiles, are not perfect, but sinners in Your sight.

Lord, when I received Christ as my Savior,
It was the end of my struggle
To be righteous by keeping the Law.

Moses wrote that if anyone could keep the Law perfectly,
And hold out against temptation,
And never break one Law,
They could be saved and appear before God,
But I could never reach that standard.

I found salvation without searching Heaven
>> To bring the physical Jesus down to me,
Nor did I descend into death to find Jesus
>> And raise Him from the dead
>> To give me eternal life.

I was saved by trusting Christ
>> And He is within reach of any who look for Him.
Everyone can have this salvation,
>> It is as easy as opening one's mouth to call for it,
>> And opening their heart to You.
Salvation is obtained by the Word of faith,
>> Which I received when I believed;
That was when I confessed with my mouth
>> That Jesus is Lord,
And believed in my heart that You raised Him from the dead;
>> I was saved!
For with my heart, I believed unto righteousness,
>> And with my mouth
>> Confession was made to salvation.

The Scriptures promise that when I believed in Christ,
>> I would not be disappointed,
>> And that is surely true.

Lord, Paul said Jews and Gentiles are the same, all must call upon You for Salvation; You are the same Lord who gives generously to those who call upon You. Paul quoted the Old Testament, "Whoever calls upon the Lord will be saved."

Lord, Paul reasoned, "How can anyone ask You to save them, unless they believe in You? How can they believe if they have never heard? How can they hear unless someone tells them? And how will anyone go preach the Gospel unless someone else sends them?"

Paul quotes the Old Testament to prove his point, "How beautiful are the feet of those who bring good tidings of good things!"

Lord, Paul was concerned that not everyone was responding to the Gospel. He quoted Isaiah, "Lord, who will believe?" Then Paul concluded, faith comes from hearing the Gospel—the Good News of Jesus' death, burial, and resurrection.

Lord, Paul was concerned about the Jews being saved; they have heard Your Word—yes—it is preached wherever the Jews live. Paul asked, "Do they understand?" Even back in Moses' time, God told the Jews, "I will use a nation—Gentiles—that is devoid of spiritual understanding to provoke you to action." Because Israel refused to preach to non-Jews, You told them, "I will be found by people who weren't looking for Me."

Lord, even while Gentiles are being saved, You still reach out Your hands to the Jews—a disobedient people—who refuse to come to You.
Amen.

## God's Mercy on the Jews

### Romans 11:1-36

Lord, Paul asked, "Has God rejected His people?" Absolutely not! Paul was a Jew, an Israelite, a descendant of Abraham, from the tribe of Benjamin. No, it is unthinkable that God has repudiated His unique people, whom He originally chose. Remember what Elijah said in the Scriptures when interceding to You for Israel, "Lord, they have killed your prophets and broken down your altars. I am the only one faithful to You, and they seek to kill me." You answered, "No, you are not the only one, I have 7,000 left who have not bowed to Baal."

Lord, in the same way, there was a remnant in Paul's day chosen by Your grace. So it was not the Jews' legalism but Your kindness that made them follow You. For if You recognized them for good works, Your grace would no longer be free.

Lord, Paul came to this conclusion, most of the Jews have not been saved—a few have found salvation—but the rest are judicially blinded, so they don't understand the Gospel. The Scriptures teach, "God has given Israel a blinded heart to this day, so that their eyes see not, and their ears hear not." David said, "The food God has provided for them has become a trap so that they think everything is well between them and God. Let their eyes be blinded to God's goodness and let them serve sin."

Lord, I realize the Jews lost their divine privileges
        Because of their sin and rejection of Your plan for them.
May I ever follow closely Your leading in my life
        And may I stay close to Your protective grace.

Lord, Paul asked the obvious question, "Have the Jews forever lost any hope of recovery? Or, have they just stumbled temporarily?" Your purpose was to make salvation available to the Gentiles, and then the Jews would be envious of what the Gentiles had, and want it for themselves. If all the world becomes rich in Your blessing because the Jews stumble, think of how much greater will be Your blessing when Jews come back to You and join the Gentiles in Christ.

Lord, You had a special message to the Gentiles and Paul constantly told this to the Jews to make them want what the Gentiles have, and thus some Jews will be saved. For if their rejection means the world is reconciled to You, how much more wonderful will be the return of Israel to You and Christ. It will be like the Jewish nation being resurrected from the dead. If the flour is good, then the bread it makes will be good, and if the root of a tree is good, then it will give good fruit. Since Abraham—the original root—was good, so eventually the nation of Israel will be children of Abraham's faith.

Lord, Paul realized the branches of the olive tree called Israel were cut off, and the Gentiles—like wild olive branches—have been grafted into Your tree. The Gentiles now enjoy the life of Your tree that gives blessing. But Gentiles should not think themselves superior, for the branches do not support the root, but the root supports the branches. Those branches—Israel—were cut off because of their unbelief.

Lord, Paul warns the Gentiles not to brag about their new superiority over Israel because they replaced the branches that were broken off. Gentiles are important because they are part of Your plan, they are branches, not the root. Gentiles may say, "Those branches were broken off so I could be grafted in," and that is true. Israel was cut off because of unbelief. But that fact should not make Gentiles proud, but fearful. If You didn't spare the natural branches—the Jews—You will not spare the Gentiles when they reject You. I won't forget, You can be severe as well as gracious. You are severe to those who reject You, and You are gracious to those who fear You, for the Jews can repent of their unbelief and be grafted back into the place of Gentiles.

Lord, you are eminently able to graft Your people—the Jews—back again. For if Your great power were able to graft wild olive branches into Your eternal plan, then it will be much easier to graft a cultivated olive branch back into its original place.

Lord, when I see Your original love for Israel,
    And I understand Your plan for Your people,
Do not forget we who are Gentiles
    And remember me, because I love You.

Lord, Paul wanted his readers to know the mystery of Your dealing with Israel, so they wouldn't be conceited. Israel is now spiritually blinded, but this will last only until the fullness of the Gentiles comes in. Then all Israel will be saved, as it is written, "The

deliverer will come from Zion, He will turn the Jews from
ungodliness, He will take away their sin."

Lord, I look forward to all Israel being saved,
    I don't know when, where or how it will happen,
But I believe You will fulfill Your promise to the Jews;
    Just remember me in your total plans for this universe.

Lord, the Jews are now enemies of the Gospel, but they are beloved as far as
    Your eternal covenant with them is concerned, because You will
    never withdraw Your gifts and calling. Remember, Gentiles were
    once rebels against You, but when the Jews rejected Jesus Christ,
    You were merciful to the Gentiles, and in the future, You will be
    merciful unto the Jews. For You have given up on all those who are
    habitually sinning, but You will also have mercy on any You choose
    to show mercy.

Lord, how rich are the depths of Your mystery,
    How deep is Your wisdom and knowledge.
I can't possibly trace Your motives
    I don't understand all that You do.
Who could ever know Your mind?
    Who could ever try to tell You what to do?
Who could ever give You anything?
    No one, for You are the Supreme God.
All that exists comes from You, and is for You;
    To You be glory forever.
                Amen.

## A Living Sacrifice to Serve God

## Romans 12:1-21

Lord, I will dedicate my body to You,
    As Paul pleaded with all believers to do.

Because of Your Mercy, I offer myself
As a living sacrifice, holy and pleasing to You;
This is the first and best spiritual worship to You.
I will not allow myself to be conformed
To the principles of this world.
But I will let my thinking be transformed
By the power of the Holy Spirit.
Then, I will discover Your will for my life,
Which will glorify You, and satisfy my desires.

Lord, because I have received grace from You,
I will not exaggerate my value or importance.
I will honestly estimate the gifts you've given me
By the standards of faith You've given me.
Just as each body has many parts,
And each part has a separate function,
So I am one part of Christ's body
Who serves in harmonious union with other believers
Because we belong to each other.
My spiritual gifts are different than other believers;
I belong to the body, i.e., to other believers
And I need all of them to help me serve You.

Lord, You've given to each one of us a spiritual gift;
This is an ability to do certain things well.
Those with the gift of prophesy, i.e., speaking for You,
Should use their gift according to their faith.
Those with the gift of helping others should serve people well,
Those with the gift of teaching should teach well.
Those with the gift of preaching,
Should do a good job delivering sermons.
Those who have been given money,
Should use it generously for spiritual projects.
Those who have the gift of administration,

Should manage everything to Your glory.
Finally, let those with the gift of mercy-showing,
    Show compassion and sympathy to the needy.

Lord, I will love everyone as You loved me,
    I will not pretend to love people when I don't.
I will seek the good things of life,
    And I will turn my back on evil things.
I will love others as your children should,
    And have deep respect for others.
I will serve You with untiring effort,
    And will be enthusiastic in all I do.
I will gladly accept all You plan for me
    And I will be patient in trouble,
    But always praying to do Your will.

Lord, when Your saints are in need,
    I will share with them the things I have
    And open my home to them.

Lord, I will always bless those who persecute me,
    And will never curse them.
I will share the happiness of those who are happy,
    And I will empathize with those who are sad.
I will treat everyone with equal kindness,
    And will not condescend to the poor.
I will not allow myself to be self-satisfied,
    But will show Christ to the world.

Lord, I will never pay back evil for evil,
    I want everyone to see my integrity.
I will try to get along with everyone,
    And be at peace with them.
I will not try to get even when someone wrongs me,
    I will leave revenge to You.

Because the Scripture teach, "Vengeance belongs to You,
>> You will pay them back for their evil."
Also the Scriptures teach, "If your enemy is hungry,
>> You must give him food,
And if Your enemy is thirsty,
>> You must give him water to drink,
>> And thus, heap hot coals on his head."
I will resist evil and conquer it by doing good.
>> Amen.

## Respect for Government

### Romans 13:1-14

Lord, I will submit to government authorities,
>> Since You have put them into office
>> And all civil authority comes from You.
Those who resist the laws of the land
>> Are rebelling against Your authority over them
>> And You will punish them.
Those who behave rightly according to Your commandments,
>> Should not be afraid of judges,
>> Only criminals have anything to fear.
I will live honestly and correctly
>> So I won't be afraid of punishment.
You put government in place to serve its citizens
>> And to carry out Your revenge on criminals,
>> Punishing them when they break the law.
I will obey the laws for my conscience sake
>> Also because I'm afraid of being punished.
This is the reason I will pay my taxes,
>> Since all officials are your officers.
I will give everyone what I owe them,

And if I owe taxes, I will pay them.
When I'm required to respect officials
     I will respect them and honor them.
I will avoid getting into debt,
          Except the debt of love I owe to all;
          When I love others, I fulfill my debt.

Lord, all the commands such as, "You shall not commit adultery," "You
     shall not kill," "You shall not steal," "You shall not covet," are
     summed up in one command, "You must love your neighbors as
     yourself." Love is the one act that will not hurt my neighbor, it's the
     only law I need.

Lord, the time has come for me to wake up
     Because the coming of the Lord Jesus is closer,
     Than when I was saved.
The night is almost over
     It will soon be daylight.
I will repent of anything
     Done under the cover of darkness,
     And put on the armor of light.
I will behave because I live in the light,
     I will not attend wild parties, nor
     Get drunk, nor commit adultery, nor get into fights.

Lord, I want you to help me live as I should,
     I will not plan to do anything evil.
                         Amen.


## Handling Questionable Things

### Romans 14:1-23

Lord, I will give a warm welcome
     To those who are weak in the faith.

I realize there are degrees of Christian obedience
>So I won't argue with any,
>>Whether or not they eat meat offered to idols.
Some believe eating meat offered to idols is all right,
>>Others who are weak in faith think it is wrong,
>>So they won't eat meat at all, just vegetables.
Those who think it is all right to eat meat,
>>Should not look down on those who don't.
And those who don't eat meat
>>Should not find fault with those who do.
You have accepted all believers as Your children,
>They are Your servants to command.
Everyone is responsible to please You,
>They are not accountable to other believers.
I will let You tell them what is right or wrong,
>You have the power to straighten out believers.
Some treat certain days holier than other days,
>>Others treat all days the same,
>>Each believer is free to hold his own convictions.
Those who observe special days
>Do so to honor You.
The one who eats meat
>>Does so to honor You,
>>If he gives thanks first.
The one who does not eat meat,
>>Also is honoring You,
>>If he gives thanks first.

I am not my own boss
>To do anything I please.
When I live, I live for You.
>>When I die, I go to be with You,
>>Whether alive or dead, I belong to You.
Christ died and was resurrected,

So that He might be the Lord of the living and the dead.
This is why I will not pass judgment on any,
> As some have done,
> Because we'll all stand before the judgment seat of Christ.

Because of this I realize that each of us
> Must give an account of ourselves to You.
For it is written in Scripture, "As I live says the Lord,
> Every knee will bow before me,
> And every tongue will confess Me."
So then, every one of us must give an account of ourselves to You.

Lord, I will not pass judgment on other believers,
> Therefore, I've made up my mind
> Never to cause my brother to stumble.
I know that food is all right to eat,
> For the Lord Jesus said, "No food is ceremonially unclean in itself."
If some think certain food is unclean,
> Then it is unclean to them.
If my attitude toward food is upsetting other believers,
> Then I will be guided by love.
I will not eat anything I choose,
> If that means the downfall of a believer
> For whom Christ has died.

Lord, I will not flaunt my spiritual privileges,
> To bring harm on another believer.
For Your Kingdom is not a matter of eating and drinking,
> But righteousness, peace, and joy in the Holy Spirit.

Lord, I will serve Christ with a respectful
> Attitude toward both eating or abstaining from food.
> Then I will please You and be respected by others.
I will adopt any custom that leads to peace,
> And the mutual respect by all believers.

I will not destroy Your work in believer's lives
   Over the question of eating and drinking,
Now all food is ceremonially clean,
   It becomes evil when I eat to make someone fall.
Therefore, my best course is to abstain from meat and wine,
   So I won't trip up a believer or weaken them.

Lord, I will hold on to my convictions,
   They are between You and me.
I will be careful when I make decisions,
   To not go against my conscience.
But any who have doubts, but eats anyway,
   Is condemned because they violate their conscience.
Anything is sin that
   Violates my faith.
       Amen.

## A Believer's Relationship to Others

### Romans 15:1-33

Lord, I believe I am a strong Christian,
   So I have a duty to bear the burdens
   Of weak Christians, lest they fall.
I will be considerate of others
   And help them become stronger Christians.
Christ didn't think only of Himself,
   Christ came to suffer from the insults
   Of those who oppose You.
I can learn from everything written in Scripture,
   For it gives me hope and an example how to live.

Lord, help me keep serving You in many ways;
   I refuse to give up.

Help me tolerate other believers
    By following the example of Christ
    Who never stopped doing good.
May I have one mind and voice,
    To give glory to the Lord Jesus Christ,
    And to praise You, the God and Father of us all.

Lord, help me glorify You by treating others
    The same way Christ treated other people.
Christ became the servant of the circumcised Jews,
    So You could carry out the promises
    You made to the patriarchs.
It was also to get Gentiles saved,
    Thus bringing glory to You.
Because the Scriptures teach, "I will worship you among
    The Gentiles, and sing praises to Your name."
In another place the Scriptures teach,
    "Rejoice ye Gentiles with His people."
And yet in another place,
    "Praise the Lord, all you Gentiles,
    And let all people praise Him."
And then Isaiah said,
    "The rest of Jesse shall appear,
    Rising up to rule the Gentiles,
    And in Him the Gentiles will hope."

Lord, may Your hope give me such power and peace,
    That the Holy Spirit will overflow me
    To remove all the barriers that hold me back.

Lord, Paul told the readers, I feel certain you have real
    Christian character and experience and that you can
    keep each other on the straight and narrow path.
    Nevertheless, Paul wrote with frankness,
    to remind them to obey truths they already knew.

Lord, Paul reminded his readers he was given a commission by You to be a minister to the Gentiles. This gave Paul a ministerial duty to tell them Your Gospel, and thus to present them as an offering to You because they are made a sweet smelling offering that You will accept.

Lord, Paul said he had a right to be proud of his work of spreading the message of Jesus Christ. Paul does not know how successful others have been but he says, "I know that I have been used by God to win the Gentiles to Christ, by the power of signs, and wonders, and by the power of the Holy Spirit." Paul tells of preaching the Good News with all his strength from Jerusalem to Illyricum.

Lord, Paul said he had a rule to never preach anywhere Christ's name was already known, lest he build on another man's foundation. Paul's chief purpose was to fulfill Scripture, "Those who have never been told about Him, will see Him; and those who have never heard will understand."

Lord, Paul explained this is why he has been prevented from coming to Rome. But since he is no longer needed in Greece, and since he has always wanted to see the believers in Rome, he planned to see them on his way to Spain. He hoped to spend some time with them, and hoped they would speed him on his journey.

Lord, Paul explained his next destination was Jerusalem to look after the Christians there. Paul was carrying money to the needy Christians there that he had collected in Northern Greece and Achaia. There Gentile Christians, took up a willing offering, even though they owed it to those in Jerusalem for sending the Gospel to them in Greece. For since the Gentiles have benefited from the Jews, it is only right that now Gentiles should look after the Jews with material things.

Lord, Paul explained he would come to them when the gift was safely
delivered to Jerusalem. Then he would come see them on his way to
Spain.

*Lord, help me be generous to all needy Christians*
*As the Christians of Greece were to those in Jerusalem.*
*Help me follow the example of Christ,*
*Who gave up everything for those most in need.*

Lord, Paul asked his readers to stand behind him in earnest prayer that he
would not fall into the hands of unbelieving Jews in Jerusalem, and
that the Jerusalem Christians will welcome his gift to them. Paul
asked these requests for the sake of the Lord Jesus Christ, and for
the love that they had for each other in the Spirit.

Lord, I pray for my life what Paul asked,
"That the God of peace be with me, Amen!"

## Greetings to Paul's Friends

### Romans 16:1-27

Lord, Paul commended Phoebe who was coming to visit the church at
Rome. She worked diligently in the Church at Cenchrea, Greece.
Paul asked them to receive her as a sister in the Lord and to help her
because she had helped many, including Paul.

Paul sent greetings to Pricilla and Aquila who had been his fellow
workers, in fact they had risked their lives for Paul. Not only is Paul
grateful for them, he says all the Gentile churches appreciate them.
Paul then greets all who worship in their home.

Paul sends greetings to Epaenetus, the first to become a Christian
in Achaia. Next Paul greets Mary, plus Andronicus and Junia his

relatives who were in prison with him. They are respected by the
apostles and were saved before Paul's conversion.

Paul next greets Amplias, Urbanus and Stachys. Then Paul greeted
Apelles who is approved by Christ and to those who work in the home
of Aristobulus. Paul sends greetings to Herodion, a relative of his,
and to the servants in Narcissus' home. He also greets Tryphena
and Tryphosa who labor in the Lord, and also to Persis.

Paul sends greets to Rufus, chosen by the Lord, and his mother who
had also been a mother to Paul. Paul also greets Asyncritus,
Phlegon, Hermas, Patrobas and the other Christians who live with
them. Paul sends greeting to Philologus, Julia, Nereus, and his
sister, plus Olympas and all the Christians who live with them.

Paul tells them to greet one another warmly because all the
churches with Paul send them greetings.

Lord, I will be on guard against anyone
    Who causes divisions in the church,
    And I will avoid them in all possible ways.
I will not be like divisive people
    Because they are a slave to their own desires.
They are not slaves to Jesus Christ,
    Because they confuse people with their arguments.

Paul wants everyone to know of the Roman believers loyal to him;
    Paul wants them to remain very loyal to the good
    And refrain from that which is evil.

Lord, You are the God of peace and harmony,
    You will soon crush satan under Your feet;
    May the grace of the Lord Jesus Christ rest on me.

Lord, Paul sent his readers greetings from Timothy, as well as
    Greetings from Jason and Sosipater. Tertius, Paul's secretary also

sends greetings. Gaius and the church that meets in his house send greetings, Erastus the treasurer of the city of Corinth and Quartus also send greetings.

Lord, I want to be strong and continually steady in my life,
    So that I give all glory to You.
I will rest in the Gospel that I heard preached,
    Because I understood the message of Jesus Christ.

This mystery of Christ and the church is now revealed to all
    But was kept secret in past ages.
Now I glory in the preaching of Jesus Christ that
    Brings all nations to obedience of faith.
Now may You the only wise God be glorified
    Through the Lord Jesus Christ, my Savior.
                  Amen.

# 1 Corinthians

## THE STORY OF WRITING
## THE BOOK OF FIRST CORINTHIANS

Date: A.D. 59 ∼ Written from: Ephesus, Turkey ∼ Written by: Paul

The sun had burst forth in her glory early in the morning and I had just finishing teaching in the school of Tyrannus. I love teaching when only believers are present.

When I first came to Ephesus, Turkey, the church met in the synagogue where Judaizers always had their negative questions because they rejected the Gospel of Jesus Christ.

But it's different in the school of Tyrannus where only believers are present. We meet in the inner courtyard of a large villa surrounded by lush gardens. When believers have questions about doctrine, I can go deeper to answer their problems. But I couldn't do it in the synagogue because I was always defending the faith.

Then came the letter from Corinth. It told of all the problems of the church in Corinth, the exact opposite of what was happening in Ephesus. The letter told of heated debates in the Corinthian church over divorce, those who never got married. The letter had concerns over speaking in tongues, eating meat offered to idols, and drunkenness at the Lord's table and theological issues at the Lord's table. I was so busy with the revival going on at Ephesus, that I didn't want to deal with a problem-driven church. But the debates were ripping apart the church at Corinth, and I had to do something.

Ephesus was having revival; people were being saved every day in this large capital city. I couldn't leave a revival to go to Corinth. I had to ask myself, *"If I left Ephesus would the Gospel continue to be spread to outlying areas?"*

There are dozens of small outlying villages where the Gospel has been aggressively preached and new churches have been established: Smyrna, Pergamus, Thyatira, Sardis, Philadelphia, and Laodicea. I rejoiced when I got word how these new churches were evangelizing other areas.

But I needed to do something for Corinth. The letter from Corinth asked about meat offered to idols. The temple of Zeus was still dominant in the city of Corinth and every butcher shop in town offered its meat to Zeus before it was sold to his customers. Christians were asking if they could eat the meat offered to Zeus, even if they didn't worship Zeus, or believe there was anything to an idol. Christians were rejecting one another—those who would not eat meat offered to idols didn't want believers in their assembly who ate meat offered to Zeus.

I shook my head as I read the letter. I began formulating a letter of response to them.

Later that day, I talked to Stephanas, Fortunatus, and Achaichus, the ones who brought the letter to me from Corinth.

Stephanas gave me an eyewitness testimony of other problems in Corinth. First, the various house churches were fussing with one another. One house church claimed superiority because they were of Paul, another claimed to be of Apollos, and a third claimed to be of Peter. Then there was an exclusive group that claimed to be the only true followers of Jesus Christ. They rejected the other house churches. I realized I needed to write on unity to the Corinthians.

Next, Fortunatus told me about the problem of human reason and philosophy. Various leaders were arguing over who was the smartest…who was right…who was wrong…. They used human reason to prove what they taught. I will write to them that wisdom comes from the Holy Spirit and that unsaved people don't have the Holy Spirit, so they don't have spiritual understanding. Even carnal Christians have difficulty understanding Christian things. Only those who were completely yielded to the Holy Spirit understand the mind of God.

Achaichus told me of another problem. There was incest in the church at Corinth that upset the people. The problem was not a clear case of incest—parent and child—but rather a man had married his father's second wife. The problem was complicated by the elders doing nothing.

And then there was another problem in the church according to Stephanas. When the various house churches argued with each other over positions of leadership, they took the issue to a secular Gentile court, "Can you imagine Christians allowing an unsaved heathen judge solving their problem of oversight in the church?"

I had to quit listening to write down the list of sins so my letter to them wouldn't omit anything. Each time I heard of another problem, I began to make some notes of what my answer would be.

Then Fortunatus told me about the problem of mass confusion at the Lord's Table. Everyone was bringing their lunch basket for a love feast, and some were even bringing alcoholic beverages and getting drunk before they came to celebrate communion. The rich had big baskets of food that they selfishly kept to themselves, while the poor had their meager rations. Then there were some who had nothing at all, and no one was sharing with them.

I again shook my head in unbelief. The Lord's Table should reflect unity in the Body of Christ when everyone breaks bread together, and when they take the cup together.

And then Achaichus told about another problem in the church. Some leaders quoted me when they spoke to the whole assembly, others would use their wisdom or quote Apollos or Peter. Then there were those who spoke in tongues claiming to have a message directly from God. I knew that tongues were necessary to validate the message of God. The New Testament Scriptures were not yet written as our authority. I wanted everyone to hear the Word of God carefully so I determined to lay down rules for the use of tongues.

And finally, Stephanas told me about the false teaching concerning the resurrection. Some were teaching there would be no resurrection in the future, but death ended it all. When I heard this, I planned to answer their question, "How can a Christian believe there will be no resurrection of their loved ones from the dead?" If they believe the Gospel, that includes the resurrection of Christ.

The day is coming to an end, and I am too tired to write. I'll be fresh to write a letter to the believers in Corinth the first thing in the morning.

*Tomorrow, I will write a letter to the Corinthians, but I must be careful to show both sides of my heart. They must feel my grief and disappointment because of their quarrellings and problems; yet, they must feel my holy indignation against their sin. I will tell them to kick the sinning Christians out of the church. Yet, I must plead for their repentance. These young Christians in Corinth need to grow in Jesus Christ.*

Sincerely yours in Christ,
Paul the apostle

# Praying the Book of First Corinthians

---
## Divisions in the Church
---

### 1 Corinthians 1:1-31

Lord, Paul introduced himself as an apostle,
    Called by the will of God
    And Sosthenes, a brother in Christ.
He wrote to Your church in Corinth
    And to all Christians everywhere.
He wrote to those Christ Jesus sanctified,
    Who pray in the name of Jesus Christ.
Paul prays for grace to all who read this letter,
    From You and from the Lord Jesus Christ.

Lord, Paul gave thanks to You for the Corinthian Christians
    Because they had been saved by grace
And they were established by knowing Christ,
    And witnessing for Him;
    And they had a full understanding of truth.
Now they were anointed by the Holy Spirit
    And had all the spiritual gifts
    As they were waiting for the return of Christ.
Paul knew You would keep them firm in faith
    And their lives would be blameless
    As they waited for the Day of the Lord Jesus Christ,
Because You are faithful to keep those
    You have called to salvation in Christ.

Lord, Paul appealed to them in the name of the Lord Jesus Christ
    To quit fussing among themselves,
But live in harmony so the Body of Christ wouldn't be ruptured,
    And there would be one unified mind in the church.
Paul had been told by those living in Chloe's house
    That the church had serious divisions.
Some are saying, "I follow Paul,"
    Others say, "I follow Apollos."
Still others maintain, "I follow Peter,"
    And some "super" spiritual claim, "I follow Christ."
Paul asked, "Have you divided Christ into many pieces?"
    Also, "Was Paul crucified for you
    So that you were baptized in Paul's name?"
Then Paul declared, "I'm glad I never baptized any of you,
    Except Crispus and Gaius;
    So none of you were baptized in my name."
Paul remembers he baptized the family of Stephanas
    But that's all he could remember.

Lord, You did not primarily send me or others to baptize people
    But to give out the Gospel to everyone.
You did not tell me to preach philosophy
    Or use "deep" words to explain Christ's death.

Lord, I know the language of the Cross is foolishness
    To those who are perishing in sin.
But I know it is Your power to save,
    Because You have saved me from a purposeless life
    And gave me understanding of spiritual matters.

Lord, Paul quoted the Scriptures that told what You said,
    "I will destroy the plans of the wise,
    Even when everyone thinks they are smart.
I will confound the intellectuals,

Then where will the earthly philosophers be?
What will happen to those who write books?"

Lord, Paul explained how average people are blinded spiritually,
So they can't find You with their wisdom.
Your plan is to save those who believe the Gospel,
Which is a "foolish" message to those who are lost.
The Jews demand miracles before they will believe;
Gentiles are looking for rational answers,
But I will preach Christ crucified,
He is a stumbling block to the Jews;
And the Gospel is foolishness to the unsaved Gentiles.
Now God has opened my eyes,
And all who are saved, whether Jew or Gentile,
Must see Christ as the catalyst of Your plan for salvation.

Lord, Your "foolishness" is wiser than all human wisdom,
Your weakness is stronger than all human strength.
When You called me I was not spiritually wise,
I thought after the pattern of ordinary people.
You did not call many influential rich,
Or highly educated people of the world,
Instead, You chose people whom the world thinks are "foolish"
To confound those the world considers smart.
Also, You chose people without influence
And those whom the world calls "low class."
You chose people hated by the world
To show up those the world thinks are brilliant
So no one can ever boast of their accomplishments,
That they had something to do with their salvation.

Lord, from You I have salvation in Christ alone
Because You have made me a member of His Body.
And by Your enablement, Christ is my wisdom,
My righteousness, my holiness, and my freedom.

As the Scriptures teach, "If any wants to boast,
>   Let him boast about what the Lord has done."
>   >   Amen.

## Understanding Spiritual Things

### 1 Corinthians 2:1-16

Lord, I will not use impressive words or philosophy
>   To give the Gospel to others.
I want everyone to know the simple message of Jesus
>   And what His death can do for them.
I will not rely on my ability to convince people
>   Because I realize how weak I am.
My speeches or sermons will not be based
>   On debate techniques or philosophy.
I want the Holy Spirit to demonstrate His power
>   In transforming the lives of those who hear the Gospel.
I don't want anyone's faith relying on human reasoning,
>   But on the power of God.
Yet, among those who know the Bible
>   I will speak with great wisdom.
Not the type of wisdom that comes from philosophers,
>   Nor the kind that appeals to "logical thinkers"
>   Whose thinking dooms them to failure,
My wisdom comes from You,
>   Telling Your plan for all people throughout the ages.
My wisdom is not understood by the great thinkers
>   For if "great men" understood Your wisdom,
>   They would never have crucified the Lord of glory.
The Scriptures explain, "No man has seen this wisdom
>   Nor have they understood God's wonderful plan
>   That He has for those who believe and love Him."

Lord, I understand Your plan for all people
> Because You sent the Holy Spirit to teach it to me.
Now the Spirit reaches into the depths of Your purpose
> To show me the things
> You hide from the world.
A person is the only one who knows for sure
> What he is thinking,
> Or what he is really like.
No one can know what You are thinking,
> Or what You are really like,
> Except the Holy Spirit reveals it to him.

Lord, You have given me the Holy Spirit
> Who is different from the spirit of this world,
> So I can understand Your gifts and plans for me.
Now I want to tell others about Your plans,
> Not using the phrases of philosophy or logic,
> But using the Holy Spirit's own words,
So those in proper fellowship with the Holy Spirit
> Can understand the spiritual meaning of Your message.

Lord, the average unsaved person can't understand Your plans,
> They sound foolish to him.
Nor can the unsaved know what the Holy Spirit is saying
> For the unsaved are spiritually blinded.

Lord, I understand Your plans for the world,
> But the unsaved person can't understand it at all.
How could they know Your plans or thoughts,
> For they can't properly pray or correctly read Scriptures;
> They are blinded to spiritual truth.
But I actually know Your purposes and plans
> Because I have Christ living in me.
> > Amen.

## Carnal Christians

### 1 Corinthians 3:1-23

Lord, Paul said he couldn't treat the Corinthians
    Like they were spiritual Christians,
    Because they were worldly and babes in Christ.
Paul didn't feed them solid food,
    Because babies can't digest solid food.
He fed them the milk of the Word—the essentials,
    Not the meat of the Word to make them strong.
Paul pointed out when they wrangled over leaders that
    They were acting like average unsaved people,
    They were motivated by the desires of the flesh.
Some in the church were proclaiming, "I am for Paul,"
    Others were yelling, "I am for Apollos."

Lord, who is Paul and who is Apollos, but Your servants
    Who preach Your Word and motivate people to faith.
They use different ways of ministering,
    Because different spiritual gifts were given them.
Paul planted and Apollos watered, but You produced growth;
    Neither the planter nor the waterer counts,
    Only You matter.
Whether they plant or water, they are a team;
    Each will be rewarded for what they do,
    We are all Your co-workers.

Lord, Paul was just the builder who laid the foundation
    On which someone else constructed the building.
That means I am building on the original foundation
    Of the Gospel and doctrine that was laid by Paul;
    Therefore, I must be careful how I work.
For no one can lay the foundation
    Because it has already been laid;

The foundation is Jesus Christ.
I will build on the foundation of Jesus Christ,
  I will use various materials of gold, silver, and jewels;
  Some will use sticks, hay, and trash.
But Judgment Day is coming
  Where our good works will be revealed.
God will use fire to judge our efforts,
  If our good works are burned up, we will be losers;
  If they stand the test, we will be rewarded.
A few Christians will have everything burned up,
  The only thing left will be their salvation.

Lord, I am Your temple, the Holy Spirit lives in me;
  I want to be holy to glorify You.
You will destroy anyone who defiles Your temple
  Because Your temple is sacred;
  My body is the temple where You desire to dwell.

Lord, don't let me deceive myself about spirituality,
  Those who think they are wise by worldly standards
Have fooled themselves
  Because the world's wisdom is folly in Your sight.
The Scriptures say, "You know men's thoughts,
  You know how futile their thoughts,"
So, I will not boast in human thinking,
  I will boast in what You've given me.
Everything You have has been given to me,
  Paul, Apollos, Peter, life, death, everything;
The present, and the future belong to You
  And I belong to Christ, and He belongs to You.
                    Amen.

## Judging Christians

### 1 Corinthians 4:1-21

Lord, I want people to think of me as Christ's servant,
    One entrusted with knowledge of You.
Now the most important thing about a servant
    Is that I, as Your servant, be found faithful.
I won't worry about what anyone thinks,
    I won't even trust my own thinking.
I have a clear conscience,
    But that is not enough to prove I'm right;
    You, Lord, alone will tell us what's right.
So, I'll not prematurely judge if anyone is good,
    I'll leave that until Christ returns,
Then all hidden things will be revealed
    And we'll know what each of us is like
    And everyone will get the reward he deserves.

Lord, Paul used himself and Apollos as an example
    So no one would play favorites;
    We must not choose one teacher over another.
The Scriptures teach, "Live by the rules,"
    Don't elevate one servant above another.
You didn't make any of us superior to another,
    You gave us the gifts we have
So no one can brag about their gifts
    As if they were superior to anyone else.

Lord, Paul rebuked the Corinthians because they wrongly thought
    They had all the spiritual things they needed.
They were acting like rich kings
    Who sit contented on their thrones.
Paul told them he wished they in fact were reigning,
    And he was reigning with them,

But that was not the fact.
Paul told them he has been appointed an apostle
    And that apostles will die for the cause of Christ.
Like prisoners on death row,
    Apostles are under the sentence of death
    And the unsaved world will rejoice in their execution.

Lord, Paul said he is foolish by the world's standards,
    But the Corinthians are claiming to be wise.
Paul said he is weak in the sight of the world,
    While the Corinthians are claiming to be strong.
Paul said the world laughs at him,
    Even as the Corinthians act like celebrities.
Lord, Paul said he goes hungry and thirsty,
    He wears rags, is brutally treated, and homeless,
    All for the cause of Christ.
Paul says he has to work hard to make money,
    Yet when he is cursed, he blesses his attackers.
    He is patient with those who injure him.
Paul said he answers quietly when insulted,
    Even when people treat him like dirt.

Lord, Paul explained he is not writing to embarrass them,
    But to warn them because they are like children.
They may have a thousand who try to teach them
    But Paul is their father in the faith,
    They were saved when he preached the Gospel to them.
That is why Paul wanted them to copy his example
    And assume the attitudes he has.
Paul plans to send Timothy to help them
    Because Paul won Timothy to Christ,
    Just as he won the Corinthians to Christ.
Timothy will teach them what Paul wants them to know,
    It's the same thing Paul taught in all the churches.

Lord, Paul realized some seized church leadership
     When he did not come to them.
So, he promised to come as soon as
     The Lord allows him.
Then Paul promised to examine the pretentious leaders
     To see if they measured up to God's standards,
Because the Kingdom of God is not talking,
     But it is power, and holiness, and obedience.
So Paul told them to decide if they want
     Him to come to punish them,
     Or to come with love and gentleness.
                              Amen.


## Influence of Evil in the Church

## 1 Corinthians 5:1-13

Lord, Paul heard reports of sexual immorality in the church
     So bad that even the unsaved won't tolerate it.
A man was living with his father's wife
     In sexual immorality.
Paul asked, "Are you so proud and blind
     That you can't see this terrible sin?"
"Shouldn't you be overwhelmed with guilt?
     You should have cast the man out of the church."

Lord, Paul said even though he was not present,
     He already knew what he would do
     Just as if he were there with them.
Call the church together to vote on this matter,
     And remember the Lord is present when you gather together.
Vote the man out of your fellowship,
     Place him in satan's hands for punishment

In the hopes his soul will be saved when Jesus returns,
    Even though he dies prematurely.

Lord, Paul rebuked their pride in their accomplishments,
    Reminding them that only a small amount of yeast
    Would influence all the dough.
Paul told them to get rid of sinful yeast
    And make the church a completely new loaf of bread,
    Remembering Christ is our Passover meal.
Paul said get rid of the sinful man,
    So they could be the unleavened bread of Passover,
    Known for sincerity and truth.

Paul reminded them he wrote a previous letter
    Telling then not to associate
    With those living immoral lives.
He explains that he didn't mean unsaved people
    Who are sexually immoral, greedy,
    Liars, thieves, and idol worshipers.
A Christian can't live in this world
    Without doing business with people like that.
What Paul meant was to disassociate
    With those claiming to be Christian
But indulge in sexual sins, including
    All the sins he just mentioned;
    Don't even eat a fellowship meal with them.

Lord, I know it's not my task to judge those outside the church,
    But it certainly is the job of believers
To hold members of the church accountable
    When they sin in the above mentioned ways.
You alone are the judge of those on the outside of the church,
    But the Corinthian Christians must deal
    With the sinning brother who disgraces Christianity,

And put him out of the church.
>Amen.

## Believer Forbidden to Go to Court Against One Another

### 1 Corinthians 6:1-20

Lord, Paul was distraught that a Corinthian believer
>Was taking a Christian matter
>Before a secular court and not before the church.
Christians will judge the world in the future
>And if the world will be judged by us,
>Why are we Christians taking cases to them?
Since Christians will one day judge angels,
>It follows we can judge one another on earth
>So why go to a judge who isn't a Christian?
You should be ashamed of yourselves,
>Isn't there someone in the church who is wise enough
>To decide these arguments?
But the Corinthian church had one brother
>Suing another in front of unbelievers.
It is embarrassing for Christians to file law suits;
>You ought to let yourselves be cheated.
Christians are wrong when they file law suits
>Because they cheat themselves out of being right.

Lord, Paul told the Corinthian believers that immoral people
>Have no share in the Kingdom of God.
This includes idol worshipers, adulterers, homosexuals,
>Thieves, greedy people, drunkards, slanderers, and swindlers.
The Corinthians committed all these sins,
>But now they are washed, cleansed, sanctified,
And saved through the name of the Lord Jesus Christ,
>And through Your Holy Spirit.

Lord, Paul said, "I can do anything I want,
      But these things are not good for me.
Even if I am allowed to do them,
      I will not become an addict to sin.
I can eat food that is meant for the stomach,
      And the stomach is created to eat food.
Don't let eating food dominate your life
      Because one day God will do away with food and the stomach."

Lord, Paul said sexual sin is never right,
      Our bodies were not created for sexual sin;
They were created as Your dwelling place;
      You, Lord, must dwell in the temple of our bodies.

Lord, I know that my body is only one member
      That makes up the Body of Christ.
That means I can't take the Body of Christ
      And join it to a prostitute. Never!
A man who has sex with a prostitute,
      Has become one body with her
Because the Scripture has stated,
      "The two shall be one flesh."
Anyone who is joined to You,
      Is one Spirit with You.

Lord, Paul warned, "Keep away from sexual sins";
      Other sins are outside the body,
      But our sexual sins are against our own body.

Lord, I will make my body the temple of the Holy Spirit
      And let Him be manifested through my body because
      I received the Holy Spirit from You.
My body does not belong to me,
      It belongs to You, Lord.
You have bought me from sin

And You paid for me with the blood of Christ,
Therefore, I will use my body to glorify You.
Amen.

## Instructions About Marriage

### 1 Corinthians 7:1-40

Lord, Paul answered the question written to him
About relationships between men and women.
"It is good for men to have
No physical contact with women."
Since immoral sex is always a temptation,
Each man should have his own wife
And each woman should have her own husband.
The husband must attend to the sexual needs of his wife,
And the wife must do the same for her husband.
The wife does not have sexual rights over her body,
The husband has those privileges.
In the same way, the husband has no sexual rights
Over his body; his wife has them.
Do not refuse sexual privileges to each other
Except for a limited time by mutual consent.
Then have the same relations as before,
So satan doesn't get an advantage over one another.

Lord, Paul said no one had to marry, but they could if they wished;
Paul wanted all men to live like him.
But each person is different in needs and desires,
God gives some the ability to be a husband or a wife,
Others have the gift of remaining single, yet being happy.

Lord, Paul told those unmarried and widows, to stay unmarried
As he is unmarried;

But if a person can't discipline himself,
>    It is better to get married than suffer.

Lord, Paul had principles for the married
>    That were not just his advice, but were Your rules.
A wife must not leave her husband;
>    If she does,
>    She must remain unmarried.
The wife must be reconciled to her husband if possible,
>    And the husband must not divorce his wife.

Lord, Paul gave the following suggestions that weren't Your commands;
>    If a Christian has an unbelieving wife,
>    And she lives peacefully with him,
>    Then he must not send her away.
If a Christian wife has an unbelieving husband,
>    And he lives peacefully with her,
>    Then she must not send him away;
Because the unbelieving husband may become a Christian
>    Through the influence of his wife,
>    And the same thing may happen to the unbelieving wife.
If there were no Christian influences from a parent
>    Then perhaps the children would not be saved,
>    But they can be saved by the influence of a believing parent.
But if an unbelieving spouse wants to separate,
>    Then the believer is not obligated to the marriage.
However, if a member of the marriage is a Christian spouse,
>    A believing wife may lead her husband to Christ,
>    And the Christian husband may lead his unbelieving wife to salvation.

Paul said his rule for all believers in the churches
>    Is to accept the situation in which God puts them.
Make sure in deciding matters about getting married
>    That they are living according to God's direction.
If a man was circumcised before he was saved,

He shouldn't disguise it.
And if anyone was uncircumcised when he was saved,
    He need not be circumcised;
Because circumcision or uncircumcision means nothing to God,
    Obeying God's commandments is what counts.

Paul told Christians to keep on doing the work
    To which God has called them.

Paul said he had no command from God
    Whether young unmarried women
    Should marry,
But Paul had an opinion
    Based on the wisdom God had given him;
Because Christians faced great danger in Paul's day,
    He felt it was best for them to remain unmarried.
Of course if a person was already married,
    They should not separate.
But if they are unmarried,
    Paul did not want them rushing into marriage.
However, if a Christian was going to get married anyway,
    They should go ahead and do it
Because marriage will bring extra problems
    That Paul didn't want them to face at the time.

Lord, I know our remaining time is short,
    So those with wives should remain
    As free as possible to serve God.
Marriage happiness or marriage disappointment
    Should not keep anyone from serving You.
Live as though there is no happiness or sadness,
    And those who live to buy things
    Should live as though they possessed nothing.
Those who have to do business in the world

Should not become attached to it
Because this world is passing away.

Lord, Paul wanted the Corinthians free from all worry
　　Because the unmarried person can devote
　　All his time to pleasing the Lord,
But the married person has to be concerned with
　　The affairs and business of this life.
They are torn in two directions—
　　Between pleasing the Lord and their spouse.
The unmarried woman can devote herself to You,
　　She is concerned about being holy in body and spirit.
The married woman has to be concerned about
　　Pleasing You and pleasing her husband.

Lord, Paul said these things to help believers be strong,
　　Not to keep them from marrying.
He wanted them to serve You as best possible
　　Without being distracted by their marriage.
If anyone feels they must marry,
　　Because they have trouble disciplining their desires,
　　They should marry; it is not a sin.
If a person has self-control, and decides not to marry,
　　Paul says they have made a wise choice.
So the one who marries is living in God's will,
　　And the one who doesn't marry can serve God better.
The wife is one with the husband, as long as he lives;
　　If he dies, she is free to marry again,
　　Only she must marry in the Lord.
In Paul's opinion, he is happier because he's not married
　　And he thinks this is God's will.
　　　　　　　　　　Amen.

## Questionable Things

### 1 Corinthians 8:1-13

Lord, Paul addressed their questions about eating food
    That was offered to idols.
Everyone thinks they have the right answer
    Because their knowledge makes them feel self-important,
    But love for others will make the church grow.
If anyone says he has all the answers,
    He is just showing how little he knows.
But the one who loves God and does His will,
    Is the one God knows.

Lord, Paul told the Corinthians that idols are just carved images,
    They are not really a god;
You are the only true God
    And nothing else is god.
Some people think there are a great number of gods
    Both in Heaven and on earth,
But I know You are the Father, the only One God,
    And that Jesus Christ created everything
    And He gives life to us.

Lord, some people don't realize that an image is not god,
    They think food offered to idols
    Is really offered to a god that lives.
So when they eat food that's been offered,
    They think they are actually worshiping that god.
But You don't care if people eat food
    That's been offered to an idol;
    You know the idol is not real or alive.
We do not sin if we eat that food,
    Nor are we better off if we refuse that food;
    Hamburger meat is nothing more than hamburger meat!

But there are some Christians whose consciences are weaker,
> They think they are recognizing or worshiping an idol
> If they eat hamburger meat that's been offered to an idol.
Here's the problem, the Christian with the weaker conscience
> May see you eat hamburger that was offered to an idol,
Then they go against their conscience to eat hamburger offered to idols,
> And they weaken their faith
> Because they think they have sinned.
So the Christian with the stronger conscience
> Who knows that hamburger is just hamburger,
> Causes the weaker Christian to damage himself.

It is a sin against Christ
> To cause a fellow Christian to stumble.
Therefore, if food offered to idols can cause a brother to sin,
> I'll not eat another hamburger for the rest of my life;
> I don't want to cause any Christian to sin against his conscience.
> Amen.

## Paul Defends His Apostleship

### 1 Corinthians 9:1-27

Lord, Paul told the Corinthians, "I am an apostle,"
> When detractors were claiming Paul wasn't an apostle.
Paul said he was not responsible to humans
> And that he actually had seen the resurrected Jesus.
Paul points out that their changed lives
> Are the results of his ministry
> And the certification of his apostolate.
Even though some Christians deny Paul is an apostle,
> Paul claims they are his authentication
> For he had won most of them to Christ.

Lord, Paul claims the right to food that You give,
      And the right to take a believing wife with him
      As do other apostles; i.e. Jesus' brother and Peter.
Then Paul asked a convicting question,
      "Must only Barnabus and I work for a living?"
Paul said he deserved to be paid because
      Soldiers are paid to serve.
Those who plant a vineyard eat of its fruit,
      And shepherds drink milk from their flocks.
While these are only illustrations, the Scriptures teach,
      "Don't put a muzzle on the ox plowing the corn."

The ploughman plows with expectation to get fed,
      And the harvester expects to get his share.
Since Paul has sown spiritual things to them,
      He expects food, shelter, and clothing in return.
The Corinthians have given to other ministers;
      Surely, Paul's rights are greater,
      Even though he hasn't exercised his rights.
Paul says he has never demanded money from them
      Because they might be less interested in the Gospel.
Those serving in the temple got their food from the temple,
      And those ministering at the altar, kept some of the food.
In the same spirit, those who preach the Gospel
      Should be financially supported by Gospel ministry.

Lord, Paul reminded the Corinthians he had not exercised his rights
      And was not writing to get money from them.
Paul said he would rather die
      Than lose the blessings of ministering for free.
But he testified he can't stop preaching the Gospel
      Since You have given him that responsibility.
Paul's greatest joy is preaching the Gospel
      Without getting paid by anyone.

Lord, I am not a slave to anyone,
>But I have made myself a slave to everyone
>So I could win as many as possible.
When I am with the Jews, I will live like the Jews
>So I can win the Jews to Christ.
When I am with Gentiles, I subject myself to their laws
>So I can win Gentiles to Christ.
When I am with heathens, who don't have any laws,
>I live among them to win them to Christ.
I don't offend the weaker Christians' conscience
>Who are bothered about meat sacrificed to idols;
>I want to win the weak to Christ.
I try to find a point of identification with all
>So I can present the Gospel message to them.
I do all this to get the Gospel to all people
>So they can come to Christ' salvation.

Lord, every runner in the race tries to win,
>But only one person gets the prize
>So I will always try to win the race for Christ.
Every fighter disciplines himself to win his awards,
>He wins a wreath that will wither;
>I want to win a prize that will never fade.
I run the race of life to win
>But it is not just to win,
>It's how I prepare and how I run.
I train hard so my body will be prepared,
>I don't want to be disqualified;
>Lord, help me win the race of life.
>>>Amen.

## Purity at the Lord's Table

### 1 Corinthians 10:1-33

Lord, may I never forget that the Jews followed the Shekinah cloud
    As they wandered in the wilderness.
You kept guiding them with the glory cloud
    And they walked safely through the Red Sea.
This is called the "baptism" for they followed Moses into the sea
    And they came out on the other side.
By a daily miracle, You sent manna to feed them
    And they drank from the rock in the desert;
    That rock was a picture of Christ to come.
Yet in spite of what you did for all of them,
    They rebelled against You and died in the wilderness.

Lord, Israel's life in the wilderness is a lesson to me,
    I will not lust after evil things,
    Nor will I worship idols as some did.
The Scriptures said not to follow their example
    For they sat down to eat the food You provided;
    Then they got up to dance and worship the golden calf.
I will never give into sexual immorality
    As some did in the wilderness
    And 23,000 died in one day.
Some of them murmured against You
    And they died of snake bites;
    Others were judged by the destroying angel.

Lord, all the things that happened in the wilderness
    Are warnings for me not to follow their example.
These negative rebellions were written as a lesson
    For me as the end of the world approaches.
When I think that I would never do these things,
    I must take heed lest I fall into their trap.

The temptations and trials that the Corinthians faced
     Are no more than I face each day.
But Lord, I know You will not let me be tempted
     With more pressures that I can overcome.
The evil desires that entice me are not any different
     Than other Christians have faced.

Lord, I know You will not let me be tempted
     Beyond my self-discipline,
But with my temptations, you'll show me how
     To overcome temptation's power.

Lord, I will avoid any idol-worship,
     I will use my common sense to avoid
     Any influence of idols in my life.

Lord, I receive a blessing from You
     When I drink the communion cup
     That represents the blood of Christ.
And I also receive a blessing when I eat the bread
     That represents the Body of Christ that was broken for me.
The single loaf represents the Body of Christ
     That even though I am only one among many,
     We form a single spiritual Body of Christ.
The Jewish people did the same thing in the Old Testament,
     They were one people when they ate together at the altar.
Does that mean when the unsaved sacrifice food to idols
     That the idols are real and alive? No!
     Does their worship have some value? No, not at all!
Those who offer food to idols are really
     Offering sacrifices to demons,
     They positively are not offering to God.
Paul said he didn't want the Corinthians
     Offering anything to demons.
A person cannot drink the communion cup of Christ

And the cup of demons at the same time,
Nor can they eat at the table of the Lord
    And the table of demons;
    Lord, don't be angry with me.

Lord, You permit me to eat all kinds of food
    But not all food is good for me,
    Nor will all kinds of food make me healthy.

Lord, I'll not spend all my time thinking of myself,
    I will be conscious of other people
    And what's best for them.
I will buy what I want in the market
    But I won't ask if it's been offered to idols
    Lest I hurt my conscience or someone else's.
Everything that comes to me from the earth
    Comes from You, and You give it to me.
If a non-Christian invites me to a meal,
    I will go eat what is served;
    I won't ask any questions for conscience's sake.
But if someone tells me that food was offered to idols,
    I won't eat it out of consideration
    For the weaker brother who stumbles at this thing.
The scruples of a weaker Christian are not mine,
    But I won't use my freedom to hurt him,
    And I won't let his conscience bind me up.
I'll eat everything with thankfulness,
    Eating it to the glory of God.
I will not cause anyone to stumble
    Whether they are Jew, Gentile, or Christian.

*Lord, I pray I won't hurt anyone at any time,*
    *I'll do what is best to get lost people saved.*
        Amen.

## Instructions About the Lord's Table

### 1 Corinthians 11:1-34

Lord, my example in all things is Christ,
    So others should follow my example as I follow Christ.
The Corinthians had done well by following
    The principles Paul taught them,
But there is one matter he wanted to re-emphasize.
    The wife is responsible to her husband,
    The husband is responsible to Christ,
    And Christ is responsible to You, the Father.
Therefore, if a man refuses to remove his hat
    When he prays or preaches the Scriptures,
    He dishonors his head—Christ.
However, a woman's hair is her honor,
    She dishonors her husband
If she prays or speaks the Scriptures without covering her head,
    She might as well have shaved her hair.
A man should not wear anything on his head
    Since he is made in the image of God,
    For a hat is a sign of rebellion to God.
God's glory is the man who is made in His image,
    And the woman is the glory of man.
The man didn't come from the woman,
    The first woman came from Adam's side.
Man was not created for woman,
    But she was created for him.
Because the angels inspect authority in the church,
    The woman must cover her head
    As a sign of authority.

Lord, I respect Your plan and purpose for men and women,
    The man and woman need each other.

Although the first woman came from Adam's side,
>Every man since then has come from a woman,
>And both men and women come from You.
Paul asked the Corinthians to use their judgment,
>Is long hair on a woman proper,
>And shouldn't she have a covering when she prays?
And isn't it foolish when men have long hair?
>But some people want to argue about this.
All Paul said was that women should be covered when praying,
>That's the way it's done in all the churches.

Lord, Paul turned his instructions to another topic;
>When the Corinthians came together for the communion service,
>They were doing more harm than good.
First, Paul said there were divisions among them
>When they came together to the Lord's Table,
And their past history of being divisive
>Made Paul believe what he heard about them.
Because each person thinks he's right,
>Each thinking they are closer to God than others.
Therefore, the Corinthians ate to honor themselves,
>Not to honor the Lord Jesus Who instituted this meal.
Some quickly eat all they could eat,
>They don't wait to share communion with one another.
Some go hungry, they don't get enough to eat,
>While the others gorge themselves
>Or they drink so much they get drunk.
Doesn't everyone have a home to eat and drink?
>They have disgraced the church,
>And embarrassed those who can't bring a lot of food.
Do you want me to praise the Corinthian church?
>Paul said, "I will not do it!"

Lord, Paul told the Corinthians You gave
      The following instruction to observe communion,
That on the night Jesus was betrayed,
      He took bread and thanked You for it.
Then He broke it and said,
      "This is My body which is broken for you.
      Eat it in remembrance of Me."
In the same way, Jesus took the cup and said,
      "This cup is the New Covenant made by God to forgive sins.
      Whenever you drink this cup, you remember Me."
Therefore, every time a believer eats this bread,
      And drinks this cup, they re-live the truth of the Gospel;
      The Lord's Table is a memorial until He comes.
Anyone who eats the bread and drinks the cup
      In an unworthily manner,
      Is guilty of sin against the Lord's body and blood.

Lord, I will therefore examine myself thoroughly
      Before eating the bread or drinking from the cup,
Because any who eats or drinks in an unworthily manner,
      Not meditating on the body and blood of Christ,
      Is contributing to his own condemnation.
That is why some Corinthians are weak or ill,
      And some have died prematurely under Your judgment.

Lord, I will carefully examine myself before communion
      So I'll not be punished or judged by You.
Yet, when a Christian is judged or punished,
      It's so he won't be condemned with the unsaved.

Lord, Paul gave them this final exhortation about communion
      That when they gather for the Lord's Table,
      They should wait for one another.
If any one is hungry, let them eat at home,
      Then the communion service will not lead

To anyone's punishment or judgment.
Paul said he would discuss other matters with them
When he arrived in Corinth.
Amen.

## Instruction About Spiritual Gifts

### 1 Corinthians 12:1-31

Lord, Paul wanted the Corinthians to know about their
Spiritual gifts that the Holy Spirit gave to each of them.
Before they were saved, they chose different idols
That couldn't say a single word.
Now there are people in the church who claim
They are speaking messages from the Spirit of God.
How can I know if their messages come from You,
Or are they just making up what they say?
Paul gave the first test—they can't claim
To speak messages from You if they curse Jesus.
The second test is that when they proclaim "Jesus is Lord,"
They are speaking Your message.

Lord, You have given many different spiritual gifts
But they all come from the Spirit of God.
These spiritual gifts are exercised in different ways,
But it's the same Spirit of God working in people.
Also, our spiritual gifts have different influences
On different people, because the Spirit of God
Uses people according to how much they yield to You,
But You are the same God working through each believer.

Lord, You give different spiritual gifts to different people
For Your own divine purposes.
You give to one the ability to preach

With great wisdom so people understand Your message.
To another, You give the ability to teach
From great knowledge so people will see many things
In the Word of God.
To another, You give faith to move mountains
And to another, You give the prayer of faith
To heal the sick of their pain and sickness.
To another, you give the ability to do miracles,
And to someone else, the power to preach and teach.
Some have the ability to recognize false spirits,
Another has the spiritual gift of speaking in tongues,
Still someone else can interpret tongues.
The Holy Spirit gives all these different spiritual gifts
To different people, just as He decides;
So believers have the ability to use these gifts
To get results in the lives of others.

Lord, just as a human body has many parts,
But all the parts make up one body,
So is the church—the Body of Christ;
Though it has many different members, it is one Body.
We have all been baptized into the Body of Christ,
Some Jews and some Gentiles; some slaves and some free.
The Holy Spirit baptized us all into Christ
And we all drink of the same salvation.

Lord, I know the body has many parts;
If the foot says "I am not a part of the body
Because I'm not the head," that does not make any difference;
That does not make him less a part of the body.
If the ear were to say, "I am not the eye,
So I'm not a part of the body,"
That would mean nothing.
If the body were all eye,

How could it hear anything?
If the body were all ears,
How could it smell anything?
But You have designed the different parts in the body.
If all the parts were the same,
How could the body function?
As it is, there are many parts of the body,
But it is still one body.
The eye cannot say to the hand,
"I do not need you."
Nor can the head say to the feet,
"I do not need you."

Lord, I know every part of the body is necessary,
But it seems the parts that are the weakest
Are the ones that are the most indispensable,
And the parts that seem to be less admirable,
Their function seems to be among the most necessary.
And the parts that are the most beautiful
Seem to be the least essential in life.
So, You have arranged to give the parts which lack importance
More dignity than the others.
So the body works together as a whole,
All the parts having the same care for others
As they have for themselves.
If one part suffers, all parts suffer with it;
If one part is honored, all parts enjoy it.

Lord, I am a member of Christ's Body,
But I am gifted differently from everyone else.
The first place was given to apostles, second to prophets,
Third to teachers and after them those who do miracles.
Next comes the gift of healing, helps, and leadership,
And last on the list is speaking in tongues.

Is everyone an apostle? Is everyone a prophet?
>Is everyone a teacher, or miracle worker or a healer?
Can everyone speak in tongues?
>And can everyone interpret them?
>The answer to these questions is "no!"

Lord, I will eagerly seek the best gifts,
>But I know love is the best gift of all.
>>Amen.

## Love Is Greatest

### 1 Corinthians 13:1-13

Lord, if I speak with the eloquence of great speakers,
>Or if I speak in the tongues of angels,
But I didn't love others, I'm simply making noise
>Like cymbals clashing or a gong that rings.
If I can predict the future, or understand Your mysteries,
>Or if I know everything, or have faith to move mountains,
>But I didn't love others, I've accomplished nothing in life.

Lord, help me always patiently express love,
>And I will find ways to be kind.
Help me never be jealous of others,
>Nor be conceited or boastful.
Help me not be irritable or resentful,
>I want my love to overlook the mistakes of others;
>I want to rejoice when others do well.
Help me love others no matter the circumstances,
>Keep my hope strong and may my love never wilt.
May my love outlast everything in life
>Because I know true love never fails.

Lord, I know the gift of prophecy will end,
　　　　And the gift of tongues will cease,
　　　　Also, knowledge will pass away,
For my knowledge is finite and imperfect,
　　　　Also, we only prophesy in part on this earth.
But when I am made perfect and complete in Heaven,
　　　　These gifts will no longer be needed.
When I was a child, I thought like a child,
　　　　Talked like a child
　　　　And my world was as small as a child's world.
In the same way, I only see things darkly
　　　　Through a stained-glass window.
But when I see Jesus face to face,
　　　　I shall understand all things fully.
Now my knowledge is partial and imperfect,
　　　　But then I shall know Jesus
　　　　As He perfectly knows me.

Lord, there are only three things
　　　　On this earth that will last:
　　　　Faith, hope, and love, and the greatest is love.
　　　　　　　　　　Amen.

## Instructions About Tongues

### 1 Corinthians 14:1-40

Lord, I want love to be my greatest spiritual gift,
　　　　But I also want the other spiritual gifts,
　　　　Especially the gift of prophecy.
Those with the gift of tongues speak to God,
　　　　But those who prophesy speak to others.
No one understands those who speak in tongues,
　　　　Because they speak the mysterious things of the Spirit.

However, those who prophesy help others grow in Christ
By motivating and instructing them.
Those with the gift of tongues benefits himself,
And those who prophecy, benefit the church.
While Paul wanted all the Corinthians
To have the gift of tongues, but
He would rather they be able to prophesy.
Unless the gift of interpretation followed tongues
no one could benefit.

Lord, Paul told the Corinthians that if he only spoke in tongues,
They would learn nothing new,
Neither would they be inspired or instructed.
Paul used a musical instrument as an illustration;
If a harp, or flute could play only one note,
Listeners couldn't appreciate one note from another,
They couldn't tell what is being played.
If no one can understand a bugle's sound
Who would be ready for battle?
If tongues do not produce an intelligible message,
Can anyone know what is being said?
He might as well be talking to the wind.
There are many different languages in the world
That are helpful to those who understand them,
But they didn't help Paul.
He said those speaking in a different language
Were foreigners to him, and he to them.
Paul wants the same principles for the Corinthians,
"Concentrate on gifts that will benefit the church."

Lord, Paul told them that if they use tongues,
Pray for someone to interpret what is being said.
Paul said if he used tongues in his prayers,
His Spirit was praying to God

But he doesn't know what he is saying.
To solve this problem, Paul said he would pray in tongues
    And he would pray in ordinary languages
    So that everyone understands and prays with him.
Paul worships God in tongues, but also with ordinary languages
    So everyone understands what he is doing.
How can the church join you in worship
    If they do not understand what you are saying?
    No matter how well you speak, the church is not benefited.
Paul thanked God that he had
    A greater gift of tongues than all of them,
But in the church he would rather speak meaningful words
    Than speak ten thousand words that no one understood.
He exhorts them not to be childish,
    But be adults in this matter.

Lord, the Scriptures say, "Through men speaking strange languages,
    And through the lips of foreigners,
    You will talk to the Gentiles
    And still they will not listen to You."
Therefore, strange tongues are a sign for unbelievers,
    Not for the believers.
While prophecy is a sign for the believers,
    Not for the unbelievers;
Otherwise a visitor coming to a church meeting
    Would think everyone was mad,
    Because they were speaking unintelligible words.
But if a visitor heard everyone speaking
    A message he could understand,
    He can be convicted by what he hears.
The visitor will have his secret thoughts exposed,
    Then he will fall on his knees, crying out to You,
    Saying, "God indeed is among the church."

Lord, Paul drew some conclusions from the above explanations:
>When the church comes together, some will sing,
>Another will preach, another will share what God said to them.

Some will use their gift of tongues, others will interpret,
>But they must do what is most beneficial to all
>And build everyone up spiritually,

Some will disagree with what Paul told them;
>He asked, "Do you think the knowledge of God
>Begins and ends with you?" Absolutely not!

Those who claim to have the gift of prophecy
>Or any other special gift from the Holy Spirit,
>Should realize Paul is giving the church Your commandment.

Paul said if anyone disagrees with this conclusion,
>He should not be recognized by the church.

In conclusion on this matter, Paul told the Corinthians to
>Desire the gift of prophecy so they could
>Explain the Word of God carefully.

Do not suppress the gift of tongues,
>Do everything decently and in order.
>>Amen.

## The Resurrection of Christ

### 1 Corinthians 15:1-58

Lord, Paul reminded the Corinthians of the content of the Gospel;
>It is the same good news he preached to them,
>They received it, and became firmly established in it.

This is the Gospel that saved them
>Unless they never originally believed it.

The first aspect of the Gospel is that Christ died for our sins,
>Just as the Scriptures teach.

He was buried and after three days,

He arose just as the Scriptures predicted.
He was seen by Peter, and then by the twelve,
>Next He appeared to 500 at the same time;
>Many are still alive and will attest to having seen Him.
Then He appeared to James, and later to all the apostles;
>Finally, He appeared to Paul.

Lord, Paul said he was the least of the apostles
>Since he persecuted the church,
>He felt unworthy to be called an apostle.
But by God's grace, Paul knew he was an apostle
>And his ministry has been fruitful.
Paul said he had worked harder than the other apostles,
>But it was Your grace, not him doing it.
What was important? Paul preached what the apostles preached,
>He preached the Gospel that saved the Corinthians.

Lord, Paul argued that if Christ were raised from the dead,
>How can any say there is no resurrection?
If there is no resurrection from the dead,
>Then Christ could not have been raised
And if Christ was not raised from the dead,
>Then Paul's preaching accomplished nothing
>And the faith of the Corinthians is useless.
Indeed, Paul has committed perjury against You, and
>The God of Heaven,
>Because he swore that You raised him from the dead.
For if the dead has not been raised,
>Then Christ was not raised from the dead.
And if Christ did not rise,
>The Corinthians are still in their sins
>And those in Christ who previously died, have perished.
If our Christian benefits are in this life only,
>We have a miserable life.

But in fact, Christ *has* been raised from the dead,
>     And is the first of millions who will live again.

Lord, Paul taught death comes through one man
>     And resurrection from the dead came through one man.
Just as all people died in Adam,
>     So, all believers will be brought to life through Christ.
However, there is an order to the resurrection:
>     Christ rose first, then when He returns,
>     All believers who have died will be raised.
After that, the end will come;
>     Christ will abolish all kingdoms, authorities, and rulers,
He will destroy every one of His enemies, of every kind,
>     Including the last enemy, death.
Then the unsaved will be raised
>     To meet their judge, Jesus Christ,
>     Who will punish them according to their sins.
When Christ finally becomes victorious over everything,
>     He will put Himself under Your authority
>     So that You will be supreme over everything.

Lord, if the dead will not be raised in the future,
>     What is the point of our getting
>     The same baptism that they got?
Why would anyone be baptized
>     If they didn't believe they would be raised?

Lord, Paul said he wouldn't continually risk himself
>     If there wasn't a resurrection.
He said he wouldn't face death daily, and fight wild beasts
>     There in Ephesus if all he got
>     Was rewarded down here on earth.
If there is no resurrection,
>     We might as well eat and drink
>     Because eventually we will die.

Lord, Paul warned them against being led astray,
      Paul said, "Bad company corrupts good living."
Paul said some of them are not even Christians
      And they should be ashamed that he had to say it.

Lord, Paul addressed their questions, "How will they be brought
      Back to life?" and "What kind of bodies will they have?"
Paul said the answer is in nature; first a seed
      Must be planted and then die in the ground;
      Then new life shall appear.
The thing that is sown is not what comes up,
      A dry little seed is planted in the ground
      And a new abundant plant comes out of the earth.
The new bush is God's plan,
      The new plant has the same life as the seed that was planted.
Not all flesh is the same kind of flesh;
      There is human flesh, animal flesh,
      Fish have flesh and so do birds.
The angels in Heaven have believed
      But their body is different than ours.
The splendor of their heavenly bodies
      Is vastly different from a human body.
The sun, moon, and stars each has its splendor,
      And each one is different from the others.
These are all illustrations of our earthly body,
      That is planted in the earth to die or decay.
But it will be raised to never decay again;
      What is planted is ugly and sickly,
      But it will be raised in glory and immortality.
Yes, the weak earthly body will be buried,
      But it will be powerful and spiritual when raised.
Just as the soul is embodied in this earthly flesh,
      Your eternal Spirit will live in our new bodies.
The first man—Adam—had a life-giving soul,

The last Adam—Christ—became a living-giving Spirit.
The first one—Adam—had a soul,
    The last one—Christ—made us eternal Spirits.
The first man was made from the dust of the earth,
    The second man came from Heaven.
Every human with a body like Adam's
    Is made of earthly dust.
Every human who is born again by Christ,
    Shall have an eternal body like Christ in Heaven.
Just as we are like Adam,
    One day we will be like Christ.

Lord, I know flesh and blood cannot enter the Kingdom of God
    Because our perishable bodies will not last forever.
It's a wonderful mystery, we shall not all die,
    But all believers will be transformed.
It will happen instantly, in the twinkling of an eye,
    When the last trumpet shall sound,
The dead in Christ will suddenly be raised,
    And the living shall all be transformed.
Our present perishable bodies will become imperishable
    And our mortal nature will be immortal.
Then the Scriptures will be fulfilled:
    "Death is swallowed up in victory.
    Death, where is your victory?
    Death, where is your sting?"

Lord, sin is the sting that causes death,
    And that sting is revealed by Your Law.
So, I thank You for victory over sin
    Through my Lord Jesus Christ.

Lord, I will do what Paul tells the Corinthians,
    I will never give in and never admit defeat.
I will keep on diligently doing Your work,

Knowing my labor is not in vain;
You will keep me safe to the resurrection.

Amen.

## Personal Greetings and Conclusion

### 1 Corinthians 16:1-24

Lord, Paul wrote to the Corinthians about needy Christians,
  Telling the readers to take up a collection for them;
  This is the same thing he told the churches in Galatia.
Each Sunday set aside some money
  According to their financial prosperity
  So Paul wouldn't need to take a collection.
Paul plans to send their offering to Jerusalem
  By those the Corinthians approved.
Those taking the offering can travel with Paul,
  If they choose to do so.
Paul told them he will come to Corinth
  And stay with them for the winter
  After he visited Northern Greece.
Paul didn't want to just "pop" in for a visit,
  He wanted to spend time with them,
  If it was "the Lord's will."

Lord, a big door of opportunity was opened to Paul in Ephesus,
  So he planned to stay there until Pentecost,
  But he was also aware of much opposition.

Lord, Paul asked the Corinthians to graciously receive Timothy
  When he visited Corinth
  So he could do Your work.
Paul directed that no one despise Timothy,
  But bless him and send him back to Paul.

Paul begged Apollos to go to Corinth,
>But Apollos adamantly refused to go at the present;
>However, he would go to Corinth in the future.

Lord, I will be aware of dangers to my faith
>And I will courageously face them.
I determine to let love motivate me
>In everything that I do.

Lord, Paul reminded the Corinthians how Stephanas' family,
>Who were the first believers in Corinth,
>Had looked after the Christian brothers.
Paul wants the Corinthians to help families
>Who have this type of ministry.
Paul told that Stephanas, Fortunatus, and Achaicus
>Had arrived in Corinth.
They have encouraged Paul in Ephesus;
>Paul wants them to appreciate these men.

Lord, Paul sends the Corinthians greetings from Aquila and Priscilla
>And the church that meets in their house;
>All the believers in Ephesus send greetings.
Paul sends them his warmest greetings,
>Wishing he could be there to embrace them.
Paul said if any does not love You, the Father,
>A curse should fall on them.
Paul prays, "May you experience the grace of the Lord Jesus";
>"My love to all in Christ Jesus."
"*Maranatha*, come quickly, Lord."
>Amen.

# 2 Corinthians

## THE STORY OF WRITING
## THE BOOK OF SECOND CORINTHIANS

Date: A.D. 60 ⁊ Written from: Philippi, Northern Greece ⁊ Written by: Paul

Titus arrived from Corinth bringing me news about the Corinthian church. My previous letters had been blunt and condemning. The Corinthians received my letter as from Christ. Those who were sinning repented. I needed that good news.

When I had written the first letter to the Corinthians, I was in the middle of a revival in Ephesus, Turkey, and couldn't leave—at least that's what I thought. But there was a great riot in Ephesus and the Christians insisted I leave for my own protection. In essence I was run out of Ephesus.

Instead of a calm voyage to Philippi where I could pray and get my thoughts together, my spirit was further upset by a vicious storm. I was shipwrecked but I escaped with my life to Philippi.

Even before reaching Philippi, I was robbed and beaten; no wonder many doubted if I had followed the will of God in this matter.

The church at Philippi was one of my favorites. I had led Lydia to Christ, a woman who sold purple cloth. Also the Philippian jailer and his family were in this church. No matter where I have gone, this church has continued to support me financially.

Titus and I sat in the courtyard of Lydia's villa where he told me what was happening in Corinth. The revival I left in Ephesus seemed to break out in Corinth. My letter had brought repentance—the church had spent whole nights in prayer—constantly begging God to forgive them.

*Lord, forgive me for my lack of faith about the Corinthian church. You have done exceedingly abundantly above all I could ask or think for the Christians in Corinth.*

Titus and I talked long about Corinth. The servants of Lydia brought us everything we needed, but most importantly, they didn't interrupt us. They could see I was writing—notes for my second letter—or we were praying.

After two days of refreshment and regaining my strength, Timothy arrived. The three of us had wonderful times of prayer.

I wanted to write to the Corinthians to let them know their letter to me was important, but that there is something greater than words on paper. I will remind them, "You are my epistle written in my heart, known and read by all people."

Next, I wanted to write and tell them to receive back the sinning brother because of his repentance. Yes, his sins were great, but when he repented and begged forgiveness, it was the duty of the Corinthians to receive him back into full fellowship.

I decided to begin the second letter to the Corinthians on the topic of comfort. I wanted them to know that the God of all comfort is the One who was comforting me now after I was run out of Ephesus, was shipwrecked, and robbed. He is the same God of comfort who will also comfort them in their problems. I will tell about all of the difficulties I had on this trip, beatings, shipwreck, robberies, and being stranded where there was no food.

I want them to know that I forgive the sinning brother, because it was not clear to me that they had forgiven their brother. I will remind them that satan gets an advantage of us for our lack of forgiveness.

Throughout the letter I will remind the Corinthians that satan is constantly attacking and that they "must be aware of his devices and tricks." I will go on to remind them, "That satan comes into their assembly with teachers denying the Gospel." I will remind them that demons can possess those who claim to be Gospel ministers. I will write, "Be careful of false teachers."

I recognized from their letter to me that the Corinthians still had problems with spiritual understanding. I had written to them in my first letter that unsaved people did not have spiritual discernment. In this letter I will remind them that "the God of this world blinds the minds of those who are not believers."

Then I will tell them that unsaved Jews have a double blindness. Their first is spiritual blindness whereby they can't understand the message of the Gospel of Jesus Christ because they are unsaved. But the Jews have a second judicial blindness because God had judged them.

The Jews told Pilate, "His blood be upon us and our children." By officially rejecting Jesus Christ, God judged them with spiritual blindness. Isaiah predicted this blindness saying, "Having eyes to see, they did not see...." That meant the Jews are blinded when they hear the message of Jesus Christ spoken in their synagogues.

I will write to them, "When the Old Testament is taught in the synagogues, Jews are blinded to teachings of Jesus with a scarf around their eyes, just as Moses had to put a veil around his face after he had seen the Lord on Mt. Sinai."

In this letter, I will again remind the Corinthians about giving money for the collection I am taking for the poor saints in Jerusalem. I will remind them that I worked hard in the shop of Aquila and Priscilla making tents so I wouldn't be a financial burden to them. Therefore, I can say, "Since I worked among you; I have the right to ask money from you to give to the poor saints in Jerusalem."

One last thing the Corinthians need to understand, they must be separated from the lust of the world. I will remind them that their bodies are the temples of God, that God no longer dwells in the temple in Jerusalem, but God dwells in their hearts.

Therefore, I will write to the Corinthians, "Come out from among worldly things and be separate, and don't touch unclean things so God can use you."

This letter must be not only tender, showing my physical weakness, weariness, and pain, but also conciliatory, that they will receive back those who had been ostracized. And if necessary, I want them to know I could still be stern if they were still in their sins when I arrive in Corinth.

I sat in the beautiful garden of Lydia to dictate this letter to the Corinthians. Titus sat at a large banquet table to write. He had stacks of paper, pen, and ink spread out before him. Timothy, who had been a pastor to the people of Corinth, sat next to me as I began. "Paul and Timothy to the believers in Corinth...." My favorite part to write was about encouragement; because God encouraged me, He could encourage them. Why? Because He is a "God of mercy and encouragement."

Sincerely yours in Christ,
The apostle Paul

# PRAYING THE BOOK OF SECOND CORINTHIANS

## Greetings to the Church

### 2 Corinthians 1:1-24

Lord, it was Your will for Paul and Timothy to write
    To the believers in the Corinthian church
    And to all Christians in the surrounding state.
May I experience grace and peace in my life
    From You, heavenly Father, and from the Lord Jesus Christ.

Lord, I bless You for encouraging me
    Because You are the Father of the Lord Jesus Christ,
    And You are the God of mercies and encouragement.
I want to encourage others who are in trouble
    With the same encouragement You gave me.
When I am greatly hurting in every area of life,
    Your promises greatly encourage me.

Lord, Paul said his suffering was for the Corinthians,
    So they could be saved and grow in grace.
Paul was hurting at the same time
    The Corinthians had great pain.
And as God was encouraging Paul to continue in ministry,
    So God would encourage the Corinthians
    To remain strong in their faith.
Paul was confident the Corinthians would remain steadfast,
    Even though they were now suffering,
    Because they were encouraged by You.

Lord, Paul didn't want to withhold his troubles from them,
So they would not be ignorant of what was happening.
That in Asia, he had intense pressures,
Greater than he ever experienced in his life,
So much that Paul thought he would die.
Paul knew that he might be killed,
But he was not trusting earthly deliverance,
Paul trusted You to raise him if he died.
Paul rejoiced that You delivered him from the threat of death,
And Paul knew that You would deliver the Corinthians.
Paul recognized that the gift of his deliverance
Came through the prayers of many Corinthians
And now they deserve credit for their intercession.

Lord, I will always follow the leading of my conscience
To treat everyone kindly and above board
Without any selfish ulterior motives.
I depend on You to help me,
That's the way Paul acted toward the Corinthians.

Paul's letters have been straight to the point,
He hasn't used worldly wisdom with them;
Paul hasn't written anything they can't understand.
Paul realizes they don't know him well
But he wants them to accept him because
When the Lord Jesus returns, they will be glad they know Christ,
Just as Paul will be glad he knows Him.

Lord, Paul told them his original plan was to visit them
Before going to Northern Greece
And then return to them after leaving Northern Greece.
Paul wanted to bless them with his ministry,
Then go on his way to Judea.
So Paul thought they may doubt his intentions
Because he did not come to them.

Paul didn't want them to think that
      He can't make up his mind.
Paul reminded them "God means what He says,
      God doesn't say 'Yes' when He means, 'No'";
      Paul knew what You wanted him to do.

Lord, You have a plan for my life;
      You faithfully fulfill Your promises to me,
      No matter how many promises there are.
I will tell everyone that You are faithful,
      Amen, glory to Your name.

Lord, You have helped me be a faithful believer
      And given me the responsibility to spread the Gospel.
You set Your seal—Your brand of ownership—on me,
      And You gave me the indwelling Holy Spirit
      As a pledge of blessings to come.

Lord, Paul swore to You that he did not come to Corinth
      Because he didn't want to rebuke them to their face,
      Or to sadden or embarrass them.
Paul said he is not their dictator
      To tell them what they must do.
Rather, he is their fellow-worker
      To make them happy and firm in the faith.
                  Amen.

## Forgive the Sinner

### 2 Corinthians 2:1-17

Lord, Paul told the Corinthians he decided not to visit them
      Because it would be painful to them.
He felt it wasn't smart to make the people miserable
      Who gave him joy;

And he couldn't be happy if they weren't happy.
Paul explained he hated to write the previous letter,
    It grieved him deeply to expose their sins.
He didn't write to hurt them,
    But he had to deal with their sins
    Because he loved them so much.
The men Paul wrote about caused great sorrow,
    So Paul had to rebuke them all
    Because they allowed sin to exist in their midst.
Paul told them one man's punishment was enough,
    He wanted them to forgive and receive him back,
    Otherwise that man may become bitter and give up.
Paul pleaded with them to show the man that
    They still loved him.

Lord, Paul explained his previous letter tested them
    To see if they were completely obedient.
Paul said he forgave anyone they forgave,
    Based on the authority of Christ's teachings.

    *When I forgive, satan doesn't get an advantage of me*
        *For I am not ignorant of his strategy;*
        *satan wants to discourage and defeat me.*

Lord, Paul told them about the open door
    In Troas to preach the Gospel,
    But Titus was not there with him.
Because Paul was worried about Titus' welfare,
    He went looking for him in Northern Greece.

Lord, I thank You for helping me triumph in Christ,
    And for using me as I spread the Gospel
    Like a sweet fragrance to motivate people to be saved.
I want to be Your fragrance everywhere I go,
    To both those who are being saved,

And to those who refuse salvation.
Because sin has the smell of death that leads to judgment,
    And the sweet fragrance of the Gospel leads to life,
    Lord, help me spread Your influence everywhere.
Therefore, I will go everywhere to spread the Gospel,
    I will speak with integrity and power.
I won't serve You, Lord, for money,
    As some are in the ministry for a salary;
Because You send me to speak for You,
    I will minister in Your sight.
                Amen.

## Instruction About Ministry

### 2 Corinthians 3:1-18

Lord, Paul said he didn't need to commend himself
    As other people needed a letter of recommendation
    When they go to meet new people.
The change in the hearts of the Corinthians
    Was Paul's letter of recommendation.
The Corinthian church is a letter written by Christ,
    Not penned with ink, nor engraved on stone,
    But written by the Spirit of the Living God.

Lord, none of us should brag about the results of our ministry,
    But we should have our confidence in Christ
    Because our ability comes from You.
You have made me a minister of the New Testament
    Which is not a written legal contract,
    But it is the inner transformation of the Holy Spirit.
Your written commandment tells me I will die
    If I try to keep the Law to be saved,
    But the Spirit gives me eternal life.

Yet, the face of Moses shone when He was given
      The commandment that led to death.
His face had such a brilliant brightness
      The Israelites couldn't look on him.
I'll experience a far greater brightness
      When I give out the Gospel by the Holy Spirit.
If the gift of the Law was glorious,
      How much more glorious the giving of the grace of God?
Actually, the Law that we thought had such great splendor
      Now seems to have none
      Compared to the splendor of Jesus Christ.
And if the Law that was temporary had some splendor,
      How much more glorious is our heavenly hope
      In Your eternal plan of salvation?
Since I know this new splendor will never cease,
      How much more boldly can I speak for You?

Lord, Moses had to put a veil over his face
      So the Israelites wouldn't see his face shining.
To this day, a veil is over the minds of Jews everywhere
      So that when the Old Testament is read,
      They can't understand what they are reading.
But when any Jew turns to You, the veil is lifted from their hearts
      So they can understand Your message.

Now Lord, Your Holy Spirit is working in hearts,
      And when the Spirit works in my life
      There is freedom to understand Your truth.
Now I, with unveiled face, look at Christ
      To see His brightness reflected
      In the mirror of the Word of God.
And constantly, I am transformed into the image of Jesus Christ
      By the work of the Spirit, Who is the Lord.
                Amen.

## Instruction About Ministry (continued)

### 2 Corinthians 4:1-18

Lord, because you have given me a great ministry
    That I didn't deserve,
I will not falsely represent myself
    Nor will I hide the truth.
I will not use tricks, nor interpret the Bible
    According to my own inclination.
But I will declare Your truth to everyone
    So they can understand Your Word.

Lord, I know lost people are spiritually blinded,
    They cannot understand the Gospel.
Satan has blinded their spiritual understanding
    To prevent them from understanding the glorious Gospel,
They cannot see Jesus Christ in Scripture
    Who is Your image.
I will not advance myself or my reputation,
    I will preach Christ Jesus, the Lord
    And I will serve those I'm trying to help;
For You Who commanded light to shine out of darkness,
    Have shined Your light into my heart
    So I see Your glory in Jesus Christ.

Lord, I have the treasure of Jesus Christ
    In my frail human body
So that outsiders will see Your power
    And know it doesn't come from my weakness.
I have troubles everywhere I go,
    But I am not distressed;
    And I don't give up.
I am persecuted, but not forsaken by You;
    I am knocked down, but not knocked out.

I face death daily, but I serve Christ Jesus
      Who went to death for sinners like me.
My life is renewed daily so others
      Can see the life of Christ shining through me.
I always faced the threat of death
      So that others can see the life of Jesus in me.
I want the faith that is described in Scripture,
      "I speak what I believe,"
May my life reflect what I speak. May I say what I believe.
      Because as You raised up the Lord Jesus from the dead,
      You'll raise me up in the last days.

Lord, Paul said he suffered so they could be saved,
      And when more are won to Christ,
      Paul will thank You more and glorify You more.
That is why Paul didn't give up
      Even when his outward body was hurting,
      His inward desire was strong to serve You.
Paul said his little troubles will pass away,
      But this short time of suffering
      Will result in Your blessing on him and them.

Lord, I will not look at my present sufferings,
      But I will look forward to being happy in Heaven,
Because things I see on earth last only for a short time,
      But the things I can't see with my physical eyes
      Are eternal—they last forever.
              Amen.

## Our Bodies Now and in Heaven

### 2 Corinthians 5:1-21

Lord, I know if my earthly body dies
    You have a spiritual body for me in Heaven,
    An eternal body made by You alone.
In this present body I groan
    As I wait for my spiritual body,
For I am not merely a spirit without a body
    Because every person has a physical body.
Yet, I groan and get weary in this body
    But it's better than not having a body at all.
Yet, when I get to Heaven I'll have a new body,
    And I won't lose this present body,
    But it will be transformed into an eternal body.
This is Your plan for me
    And You guarantee it by giving me the Holy Spirit
    To live within this body.
Therefore, I am absolutely confident
    Knowing that while I live in this earthly body,
    I am not yet in Your presence.
In this present body I must live by faith
    Which is obeying Your principles,
    Not living to please the body.

Lord, I am not afraid to die, because when this body dies,
    I'll go immediately to Your presence in Heaven.
Therefore, my aim is to please You in everything,
    Whether I'm in an earthly body or a heavenly body.
I know one day I'll stand before You to be judged
    And everything I've done will be examined,
And I'll get what my actions and thoughts deserve
    For the good or bad deeds I've done.

Lord, because I know You will judge me,
      I work hard to win people to Christ.
You know my intents and actions
      And Paul added that he hoped the Corinthians
      Also correctly knew his motives.
Paul was not making another attempt to commend himself
      To the Corinthians, but giving them reasons
      To support his ministry.
Then they would have an answer to those
      Who constantly criticize Paul.
Paul said if he was "out of place" defending himself,
      It was only to bring You glory.
And if he is making a reasonable case,
      It was for the Corinthians' sake.

Lord, the love of Christ overwhelms me when I think of His death,
      That Christ died for all sinners.
Then if He died for all, then all died with Him,
      So that I should no longer live for myself
      But for Him who died and was raised to new life.
Therefore, I will stop judging Christians
      By what the world thinks of them.
Before Paul's conversion he judged Christ only as a human,
      Now he knows Christ differently.

Because I have received Christ into my life
      You have created me a new person in Christ,
      The old life is gone, now I have a new life in Him.
My transformation is Your work,
      And I am reconciled to You through Christ,
      Now I must get others reconciled to You.
I know You worked through Christ's death
      To get the world reconciled back to You,
Now You will not punish people for their sin,

But You accept them in Christ.
Now I am Your ambassador
    To spread the message of reconciliation,
    Asking people to be "reconciled to God,"
Because You placed my sins on Christ, the Sinless One,
    And You put His righteousness on me
    So I stand perfect before You.

Amen.

## Hardship in Ministry

## 2 Corinthians 6:1-18

Lord, I want to be Your partner in ministry,
    I want everyone to take advantage
    Of Your grace that is available to all believers.
The Scriptures teach, "I, the Lord, have listened
    To my people, when they needed salvation,
    I came to them and helped them."
Now this is a good time for all people to be saved,
    Today is the day of salvation.

Lord, I will not do anything to discredit myself
    So that I make it hard for people to get saved.
Actually, I will do the opposite,
    I will do everything to bring people to Christ.

Lord, I will patiently go through sufferings
    And difficulties and pressures for You.
I am willing to be beaten, imprisoned,
    And will face angry rioters for You.
I am willing to work hard, go without sleep,
    Or go without food for You.

Lord, I want to be pure, patient, and kind,
      Loving and knowledgeable of Your principles.
So, I can minister in the Holy Spirit's power,
      According to the Word of God;
      Clothed in the armor of righteousness.
Therefore, I will stand true on the right hand and on the left,
      Prepared for honor or dishonor,
      Whether good reports or bad reports.
I will continue ministering if I'm accused of lying,
      Or, if people accept my honest presentation.
It doesn't make any difference if I'm ignored,
      Or if I'm well known.
Also, I'll continue in ministry if I narrowly escape death,
      Or if I have a safe environment.

Lord, people think my life is miserable,
      Yet, I always rejoice.
They treat me like I'm poor, and have nothing,
      But compared to all people,
      I'm rich and have everything.

Lord, Paul spoke very frankly to the Corinthians,
      He didn't hide anything from them.
The conviction they felt came from their hearts,
      It didn't come from Paul.
Paul said he spoke to them as children,
      Now he wants them to respond
      With childish enthusiasm and obedience.

Lord, I will not tie my life to the decisions
      Of unsaved people who will lead me astray;
      Good intentions can't tolerate an evil agenda.
There is no common agreement between light and darkness,
      Christ and the devil do not agree on anything.
There is no agreement between Your temple and idols,

So I won't let unbelievers control my life.
I want You to live in the body of my temple
> Because You said, "I will dwell in my people,
> Just as I dwelt in the Old Testament temple;
I will walk with them
> And they will be my people."

Lord, You want me to separate myself from unsaved people
> And not touch dirty things,
So You can welcome me and be my Father,
> And all believers shall be Your sons and daughters
> As You have promised.

Amen.

## About the Repentant Sinner

### 2 Corinthians 7:1-16

Lord, with promises as great as these,
> I will separate myself from evil,
> Whether it touches my body or spirit;
And I will be completely holy unto You,
> Living in reverence to You.

Lord, Paul asked them to keep their minds open about him
> He had not exploited anyone, hurt anyone,
> Or ruined anyone's reputation.
He was not fussing at them or blaming them
> Because they were always on his mind,
> They succeeded or failed together with him.
Paul had the highest confidence in them,
> And was encouraged by them;
> They made Paul happy in spite of his suffering.

Lord, Paul explained that he didn't get any physical rest,
>     Even when he got to Northern Greece.
There he found trouble everywhere he turned,
>     There were fightings within and fears without.
But You who encourage those who are depressed,
>     Encouraged Paul when Titus arrived.
Titus told how the Corinthians received him,
>     And were sorry for their sin,
>     And their concern for Paul.

Lord, Paul was not sorry he sent them a letter,
>     But he was sorry that the letter pained them;
>     However, they will hurt only a little while.
Now Paul is glad he sent the letter,
>     Not because he hurt them,
>     But because their pain drove them back to You.
They had a beneficial sorrow,
>     The sorrow sent by You draw Your people to Yourself.
For godly sorrow leads to repentance for salvation;
>     I will never regret this type of sorrow
>     That drives me back to You.
But worldly sorrow doesn't lead to repentance
>     But to discouragement, despondency, and death.
Paul pointed out how good was their sorrow,
>     They are now diligent to serve You;
>     They were also quick to get rid of sin.
He notes the Corinthians have completely cleaned
>     Themselves of their wrongdoings.
Therefore, Paul explains he didn't write to
>     Blame the offender, or comfort the offended,
>     But make them responsible to You.

Titus encouraged Paul when he arrived
>     To tell of their love for Paul,

And Titus was happy to bring the news.
Before Titus left to bring the letter to them,
    Paul told Titus they would repent of their sin,
    And they did not disappoint Paul.
Paul said he always told the truth,
    And his boastings of them proved true.
Paul told how Titus loved the Corinthians
    Because when he read them the letter,
    The Corinthians willingly received it with deep concern.
This made Paul happy that there was no
    Barrier between them and him;
    Now Paul has great confidence in them.
                  Amen.

## Collection for the Saints in Jerusalem

### 2 Corinthians 8:1-24

Lord, Paul wanted the Corinthians to know
    What Your grace accomplished in Northern Greece.
They in Macedonia have had difficult times
    And they have been tested with disappointments,
But they were extremely generous in giving money
    Even though they didn't have much.
Paul assured the Corinthians that the Macedonians
    Gave as much as they possibly could,
    Even more than they should.
They begged Paul to receive their offering
    So they could rejoice in helping
    The poor saints in Jerusalem.
They did more than Paul expected;
    First they gave themselves to God,
    Then they gave money to Paul for Jerusalem,

So Paul encouraged Titus to visit them
    And finish the collection of money
    That he began on a previous visit.

Lord, Paul reminded the Corinthians that they had good leaders
    And they had strong faith, good preaching
    Much knowledge, and enthusiasm.
Plus the Corinthians had a deep love for Paul,
    Now he wanted them to be leaders
    In giving joyfully to the Jerusalem project.
Paul reminded them he was not giving a command,
    But he's reminding them what others have done.

Lord, Paul reminded them of the grace of the Lord Jesus Christ
    That when He had all the riches of Heaven,
He gave up everything to help others
    So all believers could be spiritually rich
    Because of His poverty.
Therefore, Paul only suggested that the Corinthians finish
    The project, because it was they
    Who first suggested it to him.
Having begun so enthusiastically, Paul wanted them
    To finish the financial project with zeal,
    Giving whatever money they could.
Paul reminded them that God wanted them to give
    From what resources they had,
    Not from what they didn't have.
Paul also reminded them they shouldn't
    Give so much money that they suffer
    When they give to relieve the suffering of others.
Paul said suffering should be shared by all believers;
    Since the Jerusalem Christians are suffering
    Now the Corinthians can do something about it.
In the future, the Corinthians may have sufferings

And the Jerusalem Christians will help them.
The Scriptures say, "He who gathered much,
     Had nothing left over,
And he who gathered only a little bit,
     Had enough to meet his needs."

Lord, Paul was thankful that Titus had
     The same concern for the Corinthians as he had.
Titus would visit them again at Paul's suggestion,
     But Titus would have gone anyway
     Because he had deep concern for them.
Paul also sent another brother with Titus,
     Who was recognized as a good preacher
     Of the Gospel among all churches.
Paul told them this brother was elected to
     Travel with Paul to take the money to Jerusalem.
His election would prove to all the churches
     His eagerness to help the Jerusalem Christians
     And that God's grace overcomes difficulties.
By traveling together, the two would overcome
     Any rumor about how this large
     Offering would be used in Jerusalem.
Paul said, "I am trying to do right in the sight
     Of all men and of God."
To accomplish this, Paul sent a third brother
     That was well known to Paul,
The brother wanted to visit the Corinthians
     Because Paul had told him about them.

Lord, Paul said, "Tell everyone Titus is my partner
     And he is coming to help you."
"Also tell everyone the other two brothers,
     Are outstanding Christians
     And represent the churches and Paul."

Finally Paul said, "Show Your love to these men,
>And do for them what I promised you would do."
>>Amen.

## More About the Collection for the Saints in Jerusalem

### 2 Corinthians 9:1-15

Lord, Paul said he didn't need to write to the Corinthians
>About giving to needy saints,
>Because they were eager to help.
He had been boasting to the believers in Achaia
>That the Corinthians were eager to help.
>That motivated the believers in Achaia to give.
But Paul is sending the three brothers to make sure
>They give as they pledged they would.
Because if the Macedonians came with Paul
>And the Corinthians didn't give what they pledged,
>Both Paul and they would be embarrassed.
So Paul urged the three brothers to visit Corinth
>To make sure the gift is ready and waiting.

Lord, Paul wants the money to be a real gift,
>Not something that is given under pressure.
Remember, "If you give little, God's blessing will be small;
>When the farmer plants a few seeds,
>He gets small results."
"When the farmer plants a lot of seeds,
>He gets a big harvest."
Everyone must decide the budget they need to live on,
>So they will always have enough for their needs,
>And some left over to give to others.
As the Scriptures say, "He who gives to the poor,
>His gift will be remembered by God."

God, You Who give seed to the farmers, and bread
      To the hungry, will also give me what
      I need and make my harvest great.
When You make me richer in every way,
      I will be able to give generously
      And cause others to thank You.
As I give money in a Christian way,
      You supply my needs and the needs of the needy
      For this I give thanks to You.
By giving a generous gift, the Corinthians demonstrate
      Their Christian integrity,
      And those receiving the gift praise You.
Then they will pray fervently for the Corinthians
      Because they receive Your grace through them.

Lord, Paul concluded, "Thank You, Lord, for Your gift beyond words,
      The gift of Jesus Christ."
                    Amen.


## Paul Defends His Apostolic Authority

### 2 Corinthians 10:1-18

Lord, Paul appealed gently to the Corinthians about these matters,
      As compassionate as would Christ.
Yet the Corinthians are saying he is timid
      When with them, but bold in his letters.
Paul wants them to do what he asks so he
      Won't have to be harsh when he comes.
Some in Corinth think Paul is an ordinary man,
      So they don't want do what he asks or says.
Paul said, "Yes, I live as an ordinary man
      In the flesh, but I don't use the strength
      Of an ordinary man to win battles."

Paul doesn't use the weapons of the world,
  Paul uses Your power to tear down strongholds
To demolish arguments and every barrier
  Against knowledge about You
  That keeps people from finding You.
With these weapons I can capture people
  And bring them back to You
  So they become obedient to Christ.
Once the Corinthians are fully obedient to Christ,
  Then Paul is ready to punish disobedience.

Lord, Paul said the Corinthians were looking on outward things;
  To them Paul seems weak and powerless,
  But Paul tells them not to just look at the surface.
Yet, if anyone can claim the power of Christ,
  Paul says it's he.
Paul is sorry for talking too much about
  Having the authority of Christ,
But he says the Lord gave it to him,
  Not to pull down, but to build up the saints
  So he'll not apologize for using it.
Paul says he is not trying to frighten them,
  Even though some say his letters are forceful,
  But he is unimpressive in person.
They criticize that Paul's a poor preacher,
  And there's nothing authoritative about him.
Paul says those who criticize him should remember that
  What Paul is like in his letters,
  Will be what he is like in person.
Paul said he is not comparing himself
  With people who write their own "brag sheet";
  Their ego is their standard.
Rather, Paul said his standard for achievement
  Is Your divine yardstick for measuring faithfulness,

Which he followed in Corinth.
Paul said he was not overstepping his commission
    When he brought the Gospel to the Corinthians,
    Or when he exercised authority over them.
Paul said he is not taking credit for ministry
    Others have done in Corinth.
Instead, Paul hopes their faith will grow,
    Then others will appreciate what he has done.
Paul said he will be carrying the Gospel in the future
    To unreached fields; then no one will
    Criticize him for working in someone else's field.
If anyone wants to boast, let him boast in You, our Father.
    Then it's not a matter of self-approval
    But having Your approval.
                              Amen.


## False Apostles

### 2 Corinthians 11:1-33

Lord, Paul asked the Corinthians to put up with his foolishness,
    Because he is jealous over them
    With the right kind of jealousy.
Paul said, "I am concerned that the Corinthians
    Have a deep love for Christ alone,
    As a virgin bride has for her groom."
But Paul is concerned they will be led away
    From their pure love for Christ,
    As Eve was deceived by satan.
Paul said they were gullible about their faith
    Because if anyone preached another Jesus,
    That was different from the one Paul preached,
They would quickly embrace any false teacher,

Also they would quickly embrace a false spirit,
　　Different from the One they got at salvation,
Paul said those who claimed to be apostles,
　　Were no better than he was.
If Paul were a poor speaker, at least he knew
　　The message he was presenting; and
　　He had preached it many times.

Lord, Paul asked if he did wrong by not taking
　　Money from the Corinthians
　　When he preached to them.
Paul was taking money from other churches
　　To live on, so he could preach to them.
When Paul ran out of money in Corinth
　　He didn't take money from them,
　　Those who came from Philippi brought him money.
Paul said he was very careful not to burden them,
　　And he'd tell everyone the same thing in Greece,
Not to embarrass them but to
　　Cut the ground out from under those
　　Who say they minister, just as Paul does.
God never sent those false ministers;
　　They have fooled the Corinthians
　　Into thinking they are Jesus' apostles.
This didn't surprise Paul, because satan can change
　　Himself into an apostle of light,
So those who serve the devil actually
　　Appear to be godly ministers.
In the final judgment, they'll get
　　The punishment their evil deeds deserve.

Lord, Paul asked them not to think he is a fool,
　　But if the Corinthians take him as a fool
　　Paul wants to brag as a fool boasts.

Paul said the following bragging is not prompted by God,
> But is said because he has something to brag about.

The false teachers have been bragging
> Of their worldly achievements,
> So Paul will brag about his spiritual achievements.

Paul said the Corinthians had tolerated fools;
> They tolerated false teachers who made them slaves.

The false teachers made the Corinthians feed them, obey them,
> And give them all their money.

"They were slapping the Corinthians in the face."
> Paul never demanded things like that.

Yet, whatever the false teachers brag about,
> Paul has more to boast about.
> Are they Hebrews, so was Paul.
> Are they Israelites, so was Paul.
> Are they descendants of Abraham, so was Paul.
> Are they ministers of Christ, Paul said

He was foolish to even compare himself
> To them, because he was called by Christ himself.

I have served more time in prison,
> I have been beaten more times,
> I have faced death, time and again.
> I have received 39 lashes,
> Five times from the Jews.
> I have been beaten with rods five times,
> I have been stoned once.
> I have been shipwrecked three times,
> I drifted 24 hours in the sea.

I have been in danger while
> Crossing rivers, from thieves, from Jews,
> And from Gentiles.

I have been in danger in city streets,
> In the desert, on the sea, and by

False teachers.
I have experienced hard work,
> Exhaustion, sleepless nights, hunger,
> Thirst, fastings, cold and exposure.

Finally Paul said, "I have had the constant responsibility
> Of the churches. Every time someone sins,
> I have to deal with it."

"When Christians fail, I pick them up.
> When they are hurt, I comfort them."

Paul said, "I'd rather brag about my weaknesses,
> Than my accomplishments."

"God the Father of the Lord Jesus Christ,
> Knows I am telling the truth;
> Let all praise go to Him forever."

Paul told how the governor of King Aretas of Damascus,
> Tried to arrest him at the city gates,

But he was let down by a basket on a rope to escape
> Through a window in the wall.
>> Amen.

## Paul's Thorn in the Flesh

### 2 Corinthians 12:1-21

Lord, Paul said it was foolish to boast about accomplishments,
> But he has had visions and revelations from You Lord.

"Fourteen years ago I was taken to Heaven
> Whether it was physically or spiritually,
> I don't know, only God knows.

"All I know is that I was caught up into Paradise,
> (Let me repeat, I don't know if it
> Was in my body or in my spirit).

"I heard things that I cannot repeat,

I'll not brag of that experience;
    I'll brag only in my weaknesses.
"I have plenty to brag about, but I won't do it
    Because people will think I am a fool.
"I don't want people to think more highly of me
    Than they ought to think."

Lord, because Paul had this extraordinary revelation,
    You gave him a thorn in the flesh
    To keep him from getting puffed up.
Three times Paul pleaded for You to relieve
    Him from that pain,
But You told Paul, "My grace is sufficient for you
    My power will be evident in your weakness."
So Paul said, "I'll be happy to boast of my weakness
    So the power of Christ will rest on me.
"Since it is for the cause of Christ, I am
    Happy to live with my thorn in the flesh.
"I will be happy to suffer insults, hardships,
    Difficulties, and poverty
    For when I am weak, I am strong."

Lord, Paul said the Corinthians were making
    Him look foolish. They should
    Be bragging on him, not Paul bragging on himself.
Paul said he was not behind the first apostles
    In second place.
The things that characterize an apostle
    Are signs, wonders and miracles
    Which he did among the Corinthians.
These miraculous gifts meant the Corinthians
    Were not inferior to other churches.
The only thing lacking in the Corinthian church

Was they didn't pay Paul a salary;
     He asks forgiveness in this exception.

Lord, Paul told the Corinthians he was coming
     To them a third time,
And Paul said he will not take money from them,
     It is their love he wants, not their money.
Children don't take care of their parents,
     Parents take care of their children.
Paul said, "I am willing to spend my money on you,
     I will even be spent for you,
       Because I love you more than any other teacher."
Paul notes, "Some of you argue that I didn't
     Receive money from you,
But you think I tricked you,
     You think I made money off you some other way."
Paul asked them, "How did I make money?"
     Titus and the others sent Paul money,
     He didn't take money from them.
Paul noted, "We all live by the Holy Spirit,
     We all live by the same standard."
Paul explained, "You think I'm telling you these things
     To justify myself.
"Actually, I speak the truth in Christ before God,
     I say this so God will know
     I did everything for your spiritual growth."

Lord, Paul was afraid when he got to Corinth
     He would not find what he wanted to find,
And that they would not see in Paul,
     What they expected of him.
Paul was afraid he'd find arguments,
     Jealousy, hatred, divided-allegiance,
     Slander, expressions of ego and disharmony.

Paul asked them, "When I come again, will
  I be embarrassed by your behavior?
"Shall I grieve over any who have sinned,
   And are guilty of impurity,
   Yet have not repented of their evil?"
       Amen.

## Final Exhortation and Conclusion

### 2 Corinthians 13:1-14

Lord, Paul said on this his third trip to Corinth,
  He will tell them the same things
  He said on the second visit.
Now Paul is absent from them
  But he will still tell them the same things.
He repeated his authority, "At the mouth of
  Two or three witnesses
  Every word shall be established.
"I have already warned everyone,
   And especially those who are sinning, that
   I will punish them severely when I come.
"I will give you all proof
  That Christ speaks through me
  And He will not be weak in dealing with You.
"His weakened body was crucified,
  But now He has the mighty power of God.
"I am weak in my human body as He,
  But through His power I will be strong."

Lord, Paul told everyone, "Examine yourselves,
  Are you actually a Christian?
  Test yourself with this question.
"'Do you have the presence of Jesus Christ

Living in Your lives?'
"I have not failed the test,
But I have passed the test,
And I belong to Jesus Christ."

Lord, Paul prayed they would live godly lives,
Not to make him look successful,
But that God may be glorified.
Paul said his responsibility is to encourage
Them to live right at all times
And not do evil.
He was glad to be weak and despised,
If it meant they would become strong.

Lord, Paul said he hoped he wouldn't need to
Use his apostolic authority to break them,
But to lift them up.

Lord, Paul concluded, "Rejoice, grow in Christ
Live in unity, and peace, and may
The God of love and peace be with you.
"Greet one another warmly, as you should,
All the saints greet you.
"May the grace of the Lord Jesus Christ
The love of God, and presence of the Holy Spirit
Be with all of you, always."
                              Amen.

# Galatians

## THE STORY OF WRITING THE BOOK OF GALATIANS

Date: A.D. 45 ∂ Written from: Antioch, Syria ∂ Written by: Paul

It had been almost a year since Barnabas and I had completed our first missionary journey through the regions of Galatia in Turkey. Because Barnabas was the one with the strong personal relationships, he got word first of what was happening in the churches of Turkey.

Originally the Jews tried to destroy Christianity by attacking Barnabas and me physically. But now the Jews had a different strategy.

The new counter attack by the Judaizers was subtle. They wanted to undermine the foundation of Christian churches that they called a "sect." Judaizers were now infiltrating the churches to dilute the message by saying, "You must be circumcised to be saved."

I was sitting on the back patio praying when Barnabas told me about the new assault on Christians in Turkey.

"Also they deny you are an apostle," said Barnabas. "They say you may call yourself an apostle but you are not on the level of Peter and those who followed Jesus on earth."

By downgrading my authority, the Judaizers were downplaying the message of the grace of God. This way they could keep the Mosaic law and add the new teaching of Christianity. But this new Gospel is not the true gospel.

"I will write them a letter," I said, "I will set the matter straight."

"But you cannot see well enough to write," Barnabas argued with me. "You have had trouble with your eyes ever since the stoning at Lystra."

I was determined to correct the Judaizers and protect the church, so I said, "When a man must do something, God will help him." I answered, "I will squint, I will write big letters, I will write slowly and focus on each letter...but I will write."

Then I told Barnabas that the first part of my letter will justify my apostleship. I will tell them how Jesus called me, and how Jesus gave me the revelation and mysteries of God when I went into the desert.

I told Barnabas that I would add personal things that had happened to me since I saw Jesus on the Damascus Road, including the threats on my life. I will also include the fact I went to Jerusalem, but saw none of the apostles but James the Lord's brother. I will write to them that I conferred not with flesh and blood, and that I did not get my Gospel from other apostles, but from Jesus Himself.

I told Barnabas about the second part of my letter. I will tell them that both Jews and Gentiles are justified before God by faith alone. I will show how that was God's plan from the very beginning when Abraham "believed God, and it was accounted to him for righteousness."[1]

I will show that the law did not come until 430 years after Abraham was justified by faith[2] and that the Law was never intended to replace justification. I believe in the Law because it teaches us our need for Christ.[3]

Barnabas agreed with me and asked, "What about Christian living, how will you instruct them to live?"

I had already thought of the conclusion, "The result of justification by grace is spiritual freedom," I told Barnabas, no one should use their Christian freedom from the Law as an excuse to satisfy their old nature, rather freedom is an opportunity to love.[4]

Then I went on to indicate that being justified by faith does not insulate one from the struggles of life. "I will talk about the contrast between the fruits of the flesh and the fruits of the Spirit and I will show that the

Christian life is a struggle indeed, but that the Holy Spirit struggles with our old nature so that we might serve God victoriously."

The next afternoon I sat down at a table to begin writing the epistle to the Galatians. I was still agitated that the Judaizers would not recognize me so I wrote, "Paul, an apostle, not appointed by any human council, nor by any individual man, but called by Jesus Christ and God the Father."

I then said to myself, *"I am going to pray that the readers will recognize my apostleship when they read this first sentence; if they do that, they will understand what God is saying in the rest of this letter."*

I knew the Galatians were hard headed. Ethnically, the people of Galatia were from Celtic stock living in central Turkey. They were known for fierce determination, and self-discipline. They were a heady people. Politically Galatia was made a province by Rome in 25 B.C. including people from southern Turkey who were not Celtic. I knew the people well, for I was born in Tarsus in southeast Turkey. Growing up I often heard about the strong-headed Galatians across the foreboding mountains.

Barnabas and I had gone to the area on our first journey. Every time I preached in a synagogue, the Jews ran me out of town until finally in Lystra they stoned me. Whether I died is not clear, but most people who read the story say this was the occasion that I later described, "Fourteen years ago I was taken up to heaven for a visit. Don't ask me whether my body was there or just my spirit, for I don't know; only God can answer that. But anyways, while I was in paradise, I heard things so astounding that they are beyond a man's power to describe or put in words."[5]

I wrote out of white hot fervency telling them that keeping the Law never saved anyone. To the Jews the issue was circumcision, but to me the issue was becoming a "new creation" in Christ.[6] If I do not successfully argue for justification by faith alone, Christianity might become nothing more than a troublesome sect of Judaism and would be lost with the other Jewish sects.

But this commanding letter should not be taken lightly. One must agree with my conclusion that the Law does not save, and that people are saved by justification through faith alone.

Sincerely yours in Christ,
The apostle Paul

---

Martin Luther, the reformer who "jump started" the Reformation said that Galatians was "his epistle." Luther was so attached to the Book of Galatians in preaching that this book became Luther's "Magna Carta of Christian liberty" as he attacked the "religion of works" taught by the Roman Catholic church of his day.

## Endnotes

1. Gal. 3:6; Gen. 15:6.
2. Gal. 3:17.
3. Gal. 3:24-25.
4. Gal. 5:13; 6:7-10.
5. 2 Cor. 12:2-4 LB.
6. Gal. 6:15

# PRAYING THE BOOK OF GALATIANS

## The Galatians Have Departed the True Gospel

### Galatians 1:1-24

Lord, Paul wrote a letter to the Galatians, reminding them he was an
Apostle by divine commission of Jesus Christ and God the Father.
He was not appointed by any individual or by any group; therefore
they should not reject his clear teaching on salvation by grace
through faith alone.

Paul sent greetings to all the churches of Galatia, from all those
who were with him.

Paul prays for You the Father and the Lord Jesus Christ to give them
grace and peace.

Lord, I want the same grace and peace in my life
That comes only from You and the Lord Jesus Christ.
Thank You for sending Jesus to die for my sins,
To deliver me from this present evil world
According to Your eternal plans.
I give all glory to You, my heavenly Father,
And will continue to do so throughout the eternal ages.

Lord, Paul was startled that the Galatians had turned away so quickly
from the teaching of grace to follow a different gospel of works.
They no longer followed the Gospel of salvation by faith alone. They
were being blinded by those who twisted the truth of Christ into
legalism.

Lord, Paul wanted your curse on anyone who preached that salvation
comes by works. He said, "Even if an angel preached works, it
should be cursed." Then Paul repeated himself, "If anyone
preaches a Gospel contrary to what the Galatians received, let him
be under a curse forever."

Lord, Paul didn't want to please people. He wanted Your approval. If he
catered to people, he'd not be Christ's servant. That's the prayer of
my heart; I want to please You.

Lord, the Good News that Paul preached didn't come from human
thought or logic. He didn't think it up nor did anyone teach it to him.
It came by a direct revelation from Jesus Christ.

Before Paul was saved, he persecuted Christians and tried to
destroy Christianity. Paul was more zealous than most Jews his age,
and tried as diligently as possible to follow all the Jewish traditions.

But you called Paul before he was born, and chose him to be Your
apostle. Your Son was revealed to Paul so that he might preach the
Gospel of Jesus Christ to the Gentiles.

When Paul was saved, he didn't consult with anyone, and he didn't
go to Jerusalem to consult with the apostles; immediately after
Paul was saved, he went to Arabia (the desert) where You revealed
to him the doctrine of salvation by grace through faith, apart from
works. Then he returned to Damascus. Three years later, Paul went
to Jerusalem to meet Peter and stayed there 15 days. The only
other apostle that Paul met was James, our Lord's brother.

Then Paul went to minister in the provinces of Southern Turkey and
then Antioch of Syria. The churches in the Holy Land didn't even
know what Paul looked like. All they knew was, "The One who used
to persecute Christians, now preaches the faith he formerly tried to
destroy." They praised God for saving Paul.
Amen.

## The Out-Living of the In-Dwelling Christ

### Galatians 2:1-21

Lord, Paul returned to Jerusalem 14 years later accompanied by
Barnabas and Titus with definite orders from God to confront the
leaders about their false teaching that a person must be
circumcised to be saved. Paul talked privately to the leaders, telling
them that in his ministry Gentiles were being saved without
circumcision. The leaders agreed with Paul, and did not demand
that Titus who was with him be circumcised, even though Titus was a
Gentile.

Lord, Paul said the issue of Titus would not have come up, except some
false brothers had infiltrated the meeting to spy on what was
discussed. They wanted to make everyone a slave to the Old
Testament, taking away the freedom we all have in Christ.

*Lord, I thank You that I am saved by grace,*
*And that my faith is not measured by keeping the Law.*

Lord, Paul did not give in to those spying on him. He established the truth
of the Gospel for all. The leaders didn't add anything to what Paul
had said to them, or what Paul was preaching to the Gentiles.

Lord, the apostle who met with Paul accepted him as an equal (their status
didn't intimidate Paul for he knew his calling and he knew all were
equal before God). In fact, when Peter, James, and John saw the
great results Paul had preaching among the Gentiles—just as God
had used Peter to evangelize the Jews—they embraced Barnabas
and Paul. They encouraged Paul and Barnabas to continue
preaching to Gentiles, and they would continue preaching to Jews.
The only thing they added was to help the poor, which was what Paul
was already doing.

Lord, later when Peter came to Antioch, he ate his meals with Gentile
believers. But when a delegation of legalists came from James in
Jerusalem, Peter separated himself from the Gentile believers
because he was intimated by the Jews. Then some other Jewish
believers followed Peter's example by discriminating against
Gentile believers. Even Barnabas was caught up in this compromise
for a while.

Lord, when Paul realized what was happening, he said to Peter in front of
everyone, "If you are a Jew who lives like a Gentile, why do you try to
make Gentiles live like Jews?"

Lord, Paul explained: a Jew becomes a Jew by birth. A Christian becomes a
child of God by being born again. No one becomes a child of God by
keeping the Law, but a person is saved by faith in Jesus Christ. Jews
who believe in Christ become a child of God by faith in Christ and
not by obeying the Law.

Lord, no one can be saved and justified by keeping the Law;
The Jews who keep the Law are as much sinners
As Gentiles who do not keep the Law.
Does that mean Christ allows us to sin?
No! That is absurd teaching.
Paul did not try to rebuild a new system for Christians to keep the Law,
Because he taught that the legalistic system of the Law
Was done away in the death of Christ.

I died because the Law condemns all to death,
But in Christ I now live with new life.
I was crucified with Christ;
I died when He died on the Cross,
So I no longer try to live for God in the flesh.
Now Christ lives within me to give me new life;
The Christian life is the out-living of the in-dwelling Christ.

I live by the faith of the Son of God
>Who loves me and gave Himself for me.

Lord, if I could be saved by keeping the Law
>Then there was no need for Christ to die,
>And the death of Your Son was worthless.
>>Amen.

## The Law Condemns but Faith Saves Us

### Galatians 3:1-29

Lord, Paul said the Galatians were foolish because someone had blinded them to the truth of the death of Jesus Christ. Paul asked them, "Did you receive the Holy Spirit by obeying the Law?" The obvious answer is "Of course not!" Then he asked, "Are you now trying to live the Christian life by the Law after having been saved by the Holy Spirit?"

Lord, Paul reminded the Galatians that they suffered many things for the Gospel, now they were throwing it out. They were getting nothing in return for legalism.

Lord, I want the power of the Holy Spirit
>To work miracles in my life.
I know you don't do the supernatural for those living by the Law;
>You give miraculous power to live for You to those living by faith.

Lord, I know Abraham believed in You,
>And it was credited to him for righteousness;
>You looked on Abraham as though he were perfect.
I want to be a child of Abraham,
>I want to live by faith;
>I want to wholly trust You for everything.

Lord, You predicted the Gentiles would be saved by faith
      When you said, "In Abraham all the nations will be Blessed."
So I want the blessing You promised to all;
      I want You to enrich my faith.

Lord, I know those who try to keep the Law,
      Are under the curse that comes with the Law,
For legalists who don't keep all the Law
      Will be judged by the curse promised in Scripture.
No one ever got saved by obeying the Law;
      Only those living by faith will be justified.
I remember what the Scriptures teach about the Law;
      You must obey every Law without exception,
      Otherwise you are cursed by the Law.
But Christ took me out from under the curse of the Law
      When He was made a curse for me;
The Scriptures teach, "Cursed is everyone
      Who hangs on a tree."

Lord, the blessings You promised Abraham
      Come to me through faith in Jesus Christ, and
      I receive the promises of the Holy Spirit.
Now in this life a man must do what he promises,
      He cannot change his mind after he pledges his word.
God, You promised to save those who exercise faith
      So, You cannot change or cancel that promise.
God, You gave this promise to Abraham and to his seed;
      One seed—Christ, received Your promise,
      So Christ is the One saving me.
Four hundred and thirty years later You gave the Ten Commandments,
      But keeping these commandments did not save anyone,
      Because You promised Abraham salvation by faith.

Lord, You added the Law to teach us the existence of sin,
      Until the Seed came to fulfill Your promise;

Then You forgive the sin of those who exercised faith.
You gave us the Law by angels;
    The very fact You used angels proved that the Law
    Did not fulfill the promises You made to Abraham,
Because Your promise does not depend on angels,
    But it depends on Christ alone who fulfilled that promise
    Because Christ alone took away our sin.

Lord, does the Law contradict Your promise?
    No, for if the Law gave anyone spiritual life,
    Then the Law would produce righteousness.
But, the Scriptures teach all are prisoners of sin,
    The only escape is by faith in Jesus Christ
    By which I am rescued and made a Son of God.
Before Christ came, we were all prisoners of the Law
    Until the coming of Christ who freed us.
The Law was like a strict drill sergeant showing us our weaknesses
    Until we went to the school of Christ
    And learned to be justified by faith.
Once we have faith in Christ to free us,
    We don't need the Law's authority.
Now that we have faith in Christ Jesus,
    We are the children of God.
When we were baptized into Christ,
    We became a part of His family;
    We put on Christ and became like Him.
We are no longer known as a Jew or Gentile,
    A slave or free; or even men or women;
    We are all the same—we are all equal in Christ.
Since I belong to Christ, I am a descendent of Abraham;
    I am a true heir to the promises made to him.
                Amen.

## Legalism Is an Enemy of Faith

### Galatians 4:1-31

Lord, as long as the son of a rich father is a child, he doesn't have the use
of the wealth that his father has left him. When the father dies and
leaves the child an inheritance, the child has to do what his
guardian or manager tells him to do. The child is no better than a
servant in the house.

Lord, I know I am Your child and one day I'll enjoy
The riches of Heaven and perfect fellowship with You.
But, now I'll live as a slave in this present world,
I'll obey every command You give me.

Lord, before Christ came into the world, Your people were slaves to the
Jewish Law that only covered over sins. But in the fullness of time,
You sent Your Son to be born of a woman—born as a Jew—to
purchase freedom for those who were slaves to the Law. Now You
have adopted us as Your children.

Lord, I thank You that Christ Jesus was born as a Jew,
That He perfectly kept the Law,
And He nailed the Law to the Cross,
Satisfying its claims to free me;
So now I am free from its demands.

Lord, because I am Your child, You have sent the Spirit of Christ into my
heart so I can talk to You saying, "Papa, Father." I am no longer a
slave, but Your very own child. And since I am Your child, all
spiritual blessings belong to me.

Lord, before Gentiles were saved, they were slaves to idols and their manmade
gods. When they found You—or You found them—how can they
want to go back to a weak and beggarly religion and try to please
You by obeying laws? They are observing special days, and months,

and seasons to establish favor with You. They are canceling the
preaching of the Gospel that they once believed.

Lord, may I never try to please You by keeping laws
    For I am not perfect, nor can I ever be perfect;
My only plea is the blood of Christ
    Who has forgiven my sin and given me access to You.

Lord, the legalist should feel as Paul about the Law. They should be as free
    from the chains of the Law as was Paul. The Galatians did not
    despise Paul when he first preached to them, even though he was
    sick at the time. They welcomed Paul as though he were an angel
    sent from God, as though he were Christ Jesus Himself. Paul wants
    to know what happened to their gracious spirit.

Lord, may I have a good spirit about new converts
    As Paul had for the Galatians;
May I love them and pray compassionately for them
    So they will be encouraged to grow in Christ.

Lord, because of Paul's illness, the Galatians originally would have given
    their eyes to him. Now Paul wants to know why they have become
    his enemy. Legalists have taught the Galatians to live by the Law,
    but they are wrong. The legalists are attacking Paul so they can win
    the Galatians to their point of view. Paul is glad if people take an
    interest in the Galatians when their motives are good, but the
    legalists would make them slaves again to the Law.

Lord, there are some Christians who live by the Law,
    And they try to make others slaves to the Law.
Thank You that Christ has freed me from the Law;
    Now, I live free in the Kingdom of Your Son.

Lord, Paul says his children in Christ are hurting him, as though he is going
    through childbirth again for them. He is suffering till Christ be
    formed in them. Paul tells them if he were with them, he could

change their opinion. He does not like to deal with this issue by a letter. He is perplexed and doesn't know what to do.

Lord, give me grace to understand those who are misguided,
    Teach me how to relate to them.
Keep me as near to the truth as I can be,
    And may Christ always be seen in me.

Lord, Paul asked the Galatians if they really understood what the Law requires of them. They were not able to keep all of the Law, so why should they want to be under it?

Lord, I know I live in the flesh and cannot be perfect,
    I realize I cannot keep the Law.
Thank you for satisfying the demands of the Law in Your death;
    I will now live to please Christ.

Lord, Abraham had two sons, one born of a slave girl, the other born to a free woman. The son born to the slave had a natural birth, the other one was born supernaturally according to Your promise. The first woman—a slave—represented Mount Sinai, being in Arabia, the land of Ishmael, the son of the slave woman. The second woman—a free woman—represented Mount Zion in Jerusalem. This one typifies heavenly Jerusalem and is "spiritually" free from the Law.

Lord, when I was born again by the Spirit of God,
    You gave me a new nature to obey You
Which is a much greater motive to do the right things
    Than trying to keep the Law to please You.

Lord, Paul quoted Isaiah to illustrate his point,
    "Shout for joy, you barren one who bore no children,
Break into shouts of joy and gladness you who were never in labor.
    For there are more sons of the forsaken one
    Than sons of the wedded wife."

Lord, Paul told the Galatians they were like Isaac, children born of the promise. The legalists are like the child born of Hagar. Then Ishmael persecuted Isaac, which is what the Galatians are now doing to him. Paul reminded them of the Scripture, "Drive away the slave girl and her son because she should not have an inheritance with Isaac." Paul exhorts the Galatians to be children born of the free woman and not become children born to the slave woman.

*Lord, I will not put myself under the Law,*
*With all its punishments and curses;*
*I choose the freedom of living in Christ,*
*Because the Spirit of God lives in my heart.*
*Amen.*

## Characteristics of the Life of Faith

### Galatians 5:1-26

Lord, thank You that Christ freed me from the Law,
I won't be chained again to Jewish legalism,
I won't be a slave to the Law.
I won't consent again to religious laws,
I want Christ to be my freedom.
Circumcision will get no one favor with God
For if any think he must keep one law,
Then he must obey every other law.
If any tries to be justified by keeping the Law,
He cuts himself off from the life of Christ;
He has fallen from grace.
For by faith we have the hope of being righteous
And the Holy Spirit works in us to make it happen.
For in Christ—circumcision or uncircumcision—means nothing,
I must have faith which expresses itself in love.

Lord, Paul said the Galatians were growing in Christ until
    someone stopped them from obeying the truth. This wasn't from You
    because You originally called them. The Judaizers had corrupted
    them. It only takes a little leaven to influence the whole lump.

    Paul had confidence the Galatians wouldn't fall to legalism and that
    the Judaizers would be punished.

Lord, some said Paul was preaching that circumcision was necessary for
    salvation. But if that was what Paul was doing, he wouldn't be
    persecuted. The fact that Paul was being persecuted proves he was
    preaching salvation by grace through the Cross alone. Paul wanted
    the Judaizers to be cut off altogether from the Galatians.

Lord, I have been called to freedom in Christ,
    Not freedom to follow my sinful nature
    But free to serve others in love.
The Law is summed up by one commandment,
    You shall love your neighbor as yourself.
Freedom does not mean freedom to attack others
    And tear them down,
    And ruin any fellowship with them.

Lord, I will live in the Spirit
    And not satisfy the lust of my sinful nature.
All the energy of my sinful nature
    Fights against the Spirit's control,
And all the energy of the Spirit
    Fights against being controlled by my sinful nature.
These two forces are constantly fighting to control my life,
    And I feel constant pressure from both of them.
When I am controlled by the Holy Spirit,
    I am no longer a legalist.

Lord, the fruit of the sinful nature is sexual immorality,
    Impure thoughts, sensuality, worship of false gods, spiritism

(encouraging demons), hating people, attacking people, jealousy of others, and anger at everything, drunkenness, wild parties, and things like these. Those who indulge in these things will not see the Kingdom of God.

Lord, the fruit of the Spirit is love, joy, peace, patience, kindness, a
   generous spirit, faithfulness to one's word, gentleness and self-
   control. This is completely different from trying to live by the Law.

Lord, I will put to death—crucify—the lust that came
   From my sinful nature that tries to control my life.
I will live by the direction of the Spirit
   So I can fulfill the fruit of the Spirit.
I will not be ambitious for my own reputation
   So that I won't be making others jealous,
   But Christ will be the passion of my life.
                    Amen.


## The Faith-Life is a Brotherhood

### Galatians 6:1-18

Lord, when I see a fellow Christian overtaken by sin,
   I will humbly try to get them back on the right path.
I will not feel superior to them
   But will guard myself against all temptations.
I will bear the burden of other believers
   So I can obey Your commands.

Lord, when people think they are important,
   But they are really nobody,
   They end up deceiving themselves.
May every one of us do our very best in all things,
   So we can have personal satisfaction.
When we do something worth doing, then

We won't have to depend on the approval of others.
Each of us is responsible for our faults and sins,
>    For none of us is perfect.

Lord, those who teach the Word of God
>    Should be paid by those who learn from them.

Lord, no one should be deceived
>    By ignoring what You want them to do;
>    Everyone will reap the kind of crop they sow.
When someone sows to their sinful nature,
>    Their harvest will be death and destruction;
But when they sow to the Holy Spirit,
>    Their harvest will be everlasting life.
I will not get tired of doing good things
>    Because I will reap a good harvest
>    If I don't give up.
I will do good to all people
>    Every opportunity I get,
>    Especially to the household of faith.

Lord, Paul wrote with large letters because he had eye problems.
>    He warned the Galatians that the legalists were trying to become
>    popular by getting them under the Law. The legalists would be
>    persecuted if they admitted that salvation comes only by the cross
>    of Christ. Even the legalists who teach circumcision don't try to
>    keep the rest of the Law. The legalists want to boast that the
>    Galatians were their disciples.

Lord, far be it for me to glory
>    Except in the cross of our Lord Jesus Christ.
By the Cross I have put to death—crucified—the world's attractions,
>    And by the Cross I have crucified my attraction to it.
Now, it doesn't make any difference if I have been circumcised;
>    All that matters is my new desire to please You.

Lord, may Your peace and mercy be on all believers
    Who live by the power of the Spirit
    And upon all who belong to You.

Lord, Paul didn't want anyone to bother him with this issue any more. He
    had been persecuted enough with scars to prove it. Paul prayed for
    the grace of the Lord Jesus Christ to be on the Galatian believers.
                              Amen.

# Ephesians

## THE STORY OF WRITING THE BOOK OF EPHESIANS

Date: A.D. 64 ⌒ Written from: Rome, Italy ⌒ Written by: Paul

I was out for a stroll with my Roman guard; this was a privilege he gave me for the past few days. I had preached to him and he had become a believer.

However, the Roman soldier walked closely by my side and kept a hand on his sword, for if anyone killed me, that soldier might pay with his life.

I went for this walk to think about a letter I wanted to write to the church at Ephesus, so I thought a stroll along the Po River would help me focus on how to form the letter.

I wanted to write a letter to compliment the Christians in Ephesus but I didn't know how to go about it. Ephesus was a strong church that had experienced revival in the past. Of all the churches I had visited, the church in Ephesus was an example in godliness, evangelism, and service to God.

I want to write a letter complimenting them because they had taken advantage of all the benefits of living in Christ. I wanted this letter to be copied and sent to every church in the Mediterranean world. I wanted every Christian to read what a wonderful privilege it is to be a Christian. I didn't want to brag on them, lest they become proud. Also, if I bragged on individuals, the letter wouldn't be effective when read in other churches.

I prayed as I walked, "Lord speak to me, tell me what to write." Then I prayed further, "Lord, guide each word I write so that I write the truth without error."

As I walked under the shadow of the Senate building, this massive government building stood tall in the sky, reflecting the power of Rome. I was deeply impressed with the physical dominance of Rome; both in soldiers and huge government buildings surrounding the Forum. I was impressed with Rome's power, so I decided to remind the Ephesians of the power Christians have in Christ.

I thought, *"Rome is the most dominant military power on earth, but God has all power in the heavenlies."* I liked that term heavenlies and rolled it around in my mind, "the heavenlies."

So I decided to remind the Ephesians of their privilege to be citizens of Heaven. Being a citizen of Rome has many advantages, but there are more advantages of living in the heavenlies.

Everywhere, I could see the wealth of Rome: the temples...the Coliseum...huge government buildings...gold and silver everywhere. But these shows of power didn't impress me because I thought, *"In the heavenlies, God has all wealth and one day He will share it with every believer."* I'll write how wealthy Christians are in Christ.

A shopper came pushing people out of the way, and before he could reach me, the Roman soldier stepped in knocking the rude shopper down. I thought, *"That's a picture of how the Holy Spirit guards every child of God."* I thought as I continued walking, *"Even when I don't realize danger is around me, the Holy Spirit protects me, and keeps me safe."* The Ephesians need to know that when they are citizens of the heavenlies, God sends His Holy Spirit to protect them.

As we walked past a huge temple—over 100 new temples in Rome—the soldier began to tell me the differences between the greatness of Herod's temple in Jerusalem in contrast to the greatness of Rome. The soldier had served time in Jerusalem, so he said, "There's never been a rebellion in Rome, but in Jerusalem there are a couple of rebellions by renegade Jews every year."

I laughed and agreed with him, for I knew of those Jewish terrorist cells and I had seen the results of their work. Rome had been very quick to execute those who rebelled against its power.

Looking around as we walked, I saw the results of strong Roman rule. Everyone kept the laws in Rome; there was no theft, no trespassing, no rebellion. The soldier mentioned, "When in Rome, you live as a Roman but you must obey Roman laws." So I began to think of the ways I would tell the Ephesians to live for Jesus Christ. My letter would tell them how to walk as citizens of the heavenlies.

I began to compare this to the duty of a Christian to obey the Father and Jesus Christ. In every part of their life, Christians must submit to the rule of God, whether it be a wife submitting to her husband, servants submitting to their masters, or citizens submitting to their government. Then I paraphrased what the soldier had said, "Christians should live in the presence of God as God expects Christians to live."

The stroll in the sun had been good for me, thoughts crystallized themselves into the *wealth* I have as a Christian, and what God expects of my walk, and every soldier reminded me of *warfare*. By the end of my stroll, I decided that the theme of my letter to the Ephesians will be the *wealth*, *walk*, and *warfare* of believers.

Both Rome and Ephesus were capitols. Rome was capitol of the Empire, while Ephesus was capitol of all Turkey—Asia Minor. I want to point the readers away from Rome and Ephesus, I want them to know what they have in store for them in the heavenlies.

*"We live in two worlds,"* I thought. *"While we must faithfully work in this physical world, we also enjoy our blessings in the heavenly world."*

As I returned to the apartment, I said to Tychicus, "I have a task for you, something that you'll enjoy doing." Then I explained that he would be going to Turkey to deliver letters to Ephesus and Colosse. When he got there, he would read these letters to the congregations. Then the churches would copy the letters and pass them to the outlying churches.

Even though I was in chains, I felt safe in the city of Rome because I was living in the shadow of the strength of the Roman Empire. But that was physical safety. I also know that I am living in the presence of God who protects my soul. Rome only protects my body.

*"So I'll write this letter to the Christians in Ephesus, so they will take advantage of their position in Christ, as I take advantage of living in the presence of political Rome."*

Sincerely yours in Christ,
The apostle Paul

# PRAYING THE BOOK OF EPHESIANS

## Your New Standing in Grace

### Ephesians 1:1-23

Lord, Paul Your ambassador wrote this letter to believers in Ephesus who trusted You to give them spiritual victory in every part of their lives. I also want the same victory in Christ.

Lord, I want grace that comes from You the Father, and from Jesus Christ, my Savior and Lord of my life. Bless me with every spiritual blessing that comes from Heaven.

Lord, thank You for choosing me in love before the creation of the universe so that I can be holy—set aside from sin and imperfection. You chose me to enter Your presence to worship and praise You.

Lord, thank You for choosing me to be Your child according to Your plan of salvation. May I bring praise to You, Father, commensurate with the glory You already have. Christ has made me accepted by You in the grace of Your love.

Lord, my sins are forgiven through the shedding of Christ's blood. This redemption comes by the greatness of Your grace that has been lavished on all believers.

Lord, I praise You for the plan which You designed before Creation to accomplish Your will in my life and the life of every believer, so that everything in Heaven and earth will come together for the salvation of the lost.

Lord, I receive the great spiritual inheritance that You planned according to Your infinite purpose that You have for me and for each one who puts their trust in Your salvation. May I bring praise to You that is commensurate with the glory You already have.

Lord, when I heard the message of Your truth—the Gospel—that delivered me, I put my trust in You and was sealed by the Holy Spirit who guaranteed my eternal life until I come into possession of it at the rapture and thus bring You glory.

Lord, ever since I trusted in You, I've had a love for all of Your people. I have continually given thanks to You in my prayers, asking that You would give me full wisdom and understanding so I can have full knowledge of You.

Lord, I ask that You open the eyes of my heart to understand the hope to which You call me, and to see the glorious riches of my inheritance that You have given me, and to experience the greatness of Your power working in me. It's the same mighty power that raised Christ from the dead and seated Him at Your right hand, my heavenly Father, far above earthly rulers, authorities, and power in this world or in the world to come.

Lord, all things were put under Christ's feet and He was given authority over everything to benefit the church, which is His Body, the full expression of His life. Christ fills everything and Your presence is everywhere.

Amen.

## Your New Salvation

### Ephesians 2:1-22

Lord, even when I was dead in my sins, You gave me spiritual life in Christ. Before I was a Christian, my life was influenced by the world, and I was tempted by satanic powers, and I was jerked around by the rebellious spirit of people around me.

Lord, I confess I lived to fulfill the lust of the flesh, and self-advancement, and I was as rebellious as other people who are angry against You.

By You, Lord, I am rich in mercy because of Your great love for me. When I was dead in sins, You made me alive with Christ—this is Your grace that saved me—and You raised me up together with Christ, and You made me sit together with Christ in heavenly places. Then in ages to come, You will continually show me the exceeding riches of Your grace through Christ Jesus.

Lord, I am saved by grace because I put my faith in You; it was not my own doing, but Your gift to me. I cannot boast that I had anything to do with it. You have made me what I am, a new person created in Christ Jesus to serve You by doing good works, which You planned for me to do.

Lord, I remember that at one time I was a slave to my fleshly desires—the Jews who circumcised their outward flesh were no better—because we were both separated from You, heavenly Father. I was not a part of Your family, and I was not an heir to Your covenants but addicted to worldly pleasures, without hope and without Your salvation.

But now, Lord, I am united with the Lord Jesus Christ. I was far away but now I am one with Christ by His death which gave me Your peace which brought me along with all other believers into His Body. It was Christ's physical death that tore down the wall that separated people from You, the heavenly Father.

Christ, Your death satisfied the legal charges against me, and brought all believers into union with Yourself, giving me the peace of God.

Christ, by Your death on the Cross, You united everyone into one Body and brought us all back to the Father. Christ, You brought peace to those who were far away in rebellion and to those who were close but in self-righteous works. Only through You are we all able to come into the Father's presence by the Holy Spirit.

Christ, those who once were rebellious in sin are no longer foreigners or strangers, but are fellow members of Your Body with those who previously tried to save themselves by keeping the law. Both are now one building built on the foundation of the apostles and prophets, the cornerstone being You Yourself.

Christ, You hold the building together and make it grow. It is a sanctuary where Your presence dwells. Those who are Your followers are being built with other believers into a building—a sanctuary—where the Father lives by the Holy Spirit.

Amen.

## Your New Place in the Church

### Ephesians 3:1-21

Lord, Paul became a prisoner of Rome because he was first captured by Christ, the Messiah of the Jews. Paul was given this special task of evangelizing the Gentiles, and he was arrested because he persisted in preaching to Gentiles.

Lord, You gave Paul a revelation of his ministry to the Gentiles. You did not reveal the truth of preaching to Gentiles in previous generations, but now by the Holy Spirit You have revealed this task to Paul and to Your apostles and prophets.

Lord, in Your mysterious secret plan, You intended the Gentiles to share equally with the Jews in all spiritual riches that are available to Your children. The Jews and Gentiles are now one Body in Christ. Now because of what You accomplished in Your sacrificial death, both are joint heirs and joint partakers of the same body—the Church—

because of their belief in the Gospel. This is the message of grace that You gave to Paul to give to the world.

Lord, Your message was given to Paul the least deserving person in the world. Before Paul was saved, he blindly caused people to be put to death in his zeal to keep the Old Testament law. But You chose Paul to tell Gentiles about the spiritual treasures now available to them. Paul was chosen to tell everyone Your mysterious secret plan that You the Creator had hidden from the beginning. Now the riches of Your plan are seen by all, that Jews and Gentiles are joined together in Your Body, the Church. This plan was carried out through Your grace and how redemption is offered for all.

Lord, Paul has suffered because of this truth. I am not discouraged when I have to go through troubles and persecutions. Rather I am honored and encouraged that I can be a testimony to the truth.

Lord, because of my faith in You, I can come fearlessly into Your presence, knowing You will receive me and listen to my request.

Lord, because everyone is accepted in You because of Christ, I fall on my knees before You, the Father, the Creator of Heaven and earth, praying that Your power will give me inner strength through the Holy Spirit so that Christ can make His home in my heart by faith and that I'll be rooted and grounded in His love.

Lord, I also pray for the ability to understand—as all of Your children should understand—how broad, how long, how high, and how deep is Your love.

Lord, I again pray to fully experience Your love—even though it is beyond understanding—so that I can be filled with all the fullness that comes only from You.

Lord, I pray for You to work Your mighty power in me to do exceeding abundantly above all I dare to ask or think. Now to You be all glory

from ages to ages and forever!
Amen.

## Walk Worthy of Your New Position

### Ephesians 4:1-32

Lord, I want to be Your prisoner, just as was Paul. Help me live a life worthy of the calling You have given me.

Lord, I want to be humble, gentle, and patient with people, tolerating their faults; because of Your love for them and acceptance of them. Help me preserve the unity of the Holy Spirit and live peaceably with other believers.

Lord, I recognize all believers are in one body, placed there by one baptism and we all have the same calling to the one same hope.
You are the One Lord over us, we share the same one faith, one baptism and You are the only one God and Father who is in each of us, and lives through each of us.

Lord, You have given a spiritual gift to each of us according to Your generous Spirit. This is why the Scriptures say,

*After You ascended up into the heights of Heaven,*
*You led those You captured,*
*And gave spiritual gifts to all Your followers.*

The phrase, "You ascended up" means You returned to Heaven after You first came down to live and die on earth. Then You descended into the lower parts of the earth—hell—to lead Old Testament saints to Heaven. Now You rule Heaven and the entire universe.

Lord, You gave spiritual gifts to Your followers; some apostles, some prophets, some evangelists, and some shepherd-teachers. Their duty is to equip Your people to do Your work and build up the Body,

166

Your Church, until we all become united in faith and knowledge of Your will, so that each of us grows to full maturity, according to the standard You have set up.

Lord, I know my standard is to become like Christ.

Lord, I don't want to be like a child, always changing my mind about what I believe because someone tells me different things, or because someone misleads me. Instead, help me hold on to the truth in love, growing more like You every day, because You are the head of all of us, You are over the Body where we are members. Under Your direction, each part of the Body will help others grow so that all of us become mature believers, and the whole Body becomes mature in love for one another.

Lord, I will no longer live the way the ungodly live, because they do not understand Your ways. Their minds are spiritually blinded and they are far away from You the Father because they have shut their minds to the truth and resisted Your will. They don't care about doing right but have given themselves to immorality. Their lives are filled with filthiness and greed.

Lord, that is not the way You taught me to live. You told me to put off the old evil nature, because it is thoroughly filled with lust and lying. You told me to be spiritually renewed in my thoughts and attitudes so that I put on the new nature which You created to be godly, righteous, and holy.

Lord, I will put away lying, and I will tell everyone the truth because we are related to one another in Your Body. I will stop being angry and sinning against others, and I will not let the sun go down on my wrath because anger gives room for the enemy to get into my life.

Lord, the thief must stop stealing and work for an honest living, then give to those who have needs.

Lord, the curser must stop using foul language. He must only allow good
words to come from his mouth that are helpful to those who hear him.

Lord, I will not give grief to the Holy Spirit by living a sinful life, because
He has sealed me with the authority of His presence
that will keep me until the final day of redemption.

Lord, I will get rid of all bitterness, rage, name calling, mean-spirited words
and slander, along with spiteful retaliation. Instead, I will be kind to
others, tenderhearted, forgiving others as You, Father, forgave me,
because of Christ.
Amen.

## Walk Worthy as Children of God

### Ephesians 5:1-33

Lord, I will follow You as a child follows his parents because I am Your
child. I will walk in love to others as Christ loved me and
demonstrated it by giving Himself as a sweet and acceptable
sacrifice to You, my Father.

Lord, I will not be involved in sexual sins or dirty actions or greediness
because those things are contrary to godliness. Also, I will not be
known by filthy speech, foolish talking, and jesting, but I will be
gracious in all things.

Lord, I know there is no place in Your Kingdom for those who are sexually
addicted, nor for the filthy minded, nor for greedy people. No matter
how much people excuse these sins, You, Father, will still punish
them, as You will all those who are disobedient. Therefore, I will not
get involved in those things.

Lord, in the past I walked in darkness, but now I have Your light; I will walk
in Your light.

Lord, I want the fruit of the Spirit in my life; I want to be good and do what is right, and tell the truth so I can be acceptable to You.

Lord, I will not have anything to do with the works of darkness, rather I will expose them, remembering it is shameful to speak of the things people do in secret. But when light shines on them, their deeds are clearly revealed for what they are. This is why it is said:

*Awake, sleeper, get up from the dead;*
*And Christ will give you light.*

Therefore Lord, I will be careful how I live my life, not as a fool but as a wise person. I will use my time wisely because these are evil days. I will not be foolish, but will try to understand Your will for my life.

Lord, I won't drink wine, because I will lose control of myself. Instead I will let the Holy Spirit continually fill me and control me. Then I'll sing psalms, hymns, and spiritual songs with other believers, making music in my heart to You.

Lord, I will continually give thanks for everything to You, the Father, in the name of my Lord Jesus Christ.

Lord, I will submit myself to other believers out of reverence to You. I know wives should submit to their own husbands, just as they do to You. For the husband is the head of the wife, just as Christ is the head of the Body and is its Savior. Just as the Body submits to Christ as its head, so also wives should submit to their husband in everything.

Lord, husbands should love their wives, just as Christ loved the Church and gave His life to make it holy and clean, through washing of the Word of God. Christ did this to make the Church glorious, without spot, wrinkle, or blemish. Husbands should love their wives as they love their bodies, because a man is actually looking out for himself when he loves his wife. No one hates his body. On the contrary, a man will feed and care for his body, just as Christ cares for His Body, the Church.

Lord, the Scriptures teach that a man should leave his father and mother to be joined to his wife and the two become one. This is a great mystery; but it illustrates the relationship between Christ and the Church. So each man must love his wife the way he loves himself and the wife must respect her husband.

Amen.

## Your Spiritual Warfare as a Believer

### Ephesians 6:1-24

Lord, children should obey their parents because they belong to You, for this is what You want them to do. One of the Ten Commandments has a promise stating, "Honor your father and mother so that it will go well with you and you will live a long and prosperous life."

Lord, You don't want fathers to irritate their children because it makes them resentful. Rather, You want fathers to bring them up with positive discipline that You approve.

Lord, You want workers to obey and respect their employers, and fear displeasing their bosses, just as they would fear displeasing You. They shouldn't work hard just to "butter up the boss" when he's watching, but they should put passion into their work as though working for You; because You will reward everyone for their good service, whether they're a boss or worker. And bosses must treat their workers right, not threaten them because both bosses and employees work for You, and You have no favorites.

Lord, I will be strong in Your power and put on all the spiritual armor so I can stand against the deceptive strategy of the enemy. I am not fighting against humans who have flesh and blood, but against evil

powers, authorities, and demons of the unseen world; and I'm
struggling against the mighty powers of darkness and their tricks.
I'm fighting against filthy spirits who influence this world from their
ethereal realm.

Lord, I'll use every piece of Your armor so that when evil comes, I'll be able
to resist and win the battle. With Your help, I'll stand in battle with
Your truth buckled around my waist. I'll cover my chest with the
armor of righteousness, and I'll wear the shoes of peace that come
from the good news of the Gospel. I'll carry the shield of faith to
stop all the arrows and fiery darts of the evil one. I'll wear the
protective helmet of salvation and I'll protect myself with the sword
of the Spirit, which is the Word of God.

Lord, I will pray at all times, with every type of intercession and spiritual
warfare. I will pray persistently and boldly for all
Christians everywhere.

Lord, I will pray for those who minister for You so they will have boldness
and the right words to proclaim the message of the good news of the
Gospel. This was Paul's request and the reason why he was in
chains in Rome. Just as Paul prayed for strength to keep on sharing
the Gospel, that is my prayer for me and for all your ministers.

Lord, Tychicus delivered this letter to the saints on Ephesus and told them
all about Paul so they would be encouraged.

Lord, I want Your peace ruling my heart, and so give me a deep love to live
for You. I want Your grace in my life and on all those who love You
deeply with an enduring love.
Amen.

# Philippians

## THE STORY OF WRITING
## THE BOOK OF PHILIPPIANS

Date: A.D. 64 ∼ Written from: Rome, Italy ∼ Written by: Paul

Yesterday, Epaphroditus arrived in Rome bringing a large financial gift to me and the others from the church in Philippi. We needed the money because there are several of us living in this apartment and we feed many soldiers and guest visitors.

Theophilus originally had given a large gift to Luke for the writing of the Book of Acts, but it was beginning to run out. I knew God would take care of our needs and God heard our request before the money arrived from Philippi.

"I must write and thank them for their gift," I told Silas and Timothy.

The day was sunny and a warm breeze found its way between the buildings and into our apartment. The bitter winds of winter were gone, and each day the sun climbed higher in the heavens. That meant each day more of the sun found its way into our apartment. I could smell spring in the air, the plants in the window pots were beginning to sprout new leaves.

"It's a great day to be alive," I told Luke. But one of the realists reminded me,

"Don't forget, you are still one of Nero's prisoners, you're still in chains, and there is a guard at the door who watches everything you do."

"Yes...but we have Christ...and the weather is comfortable...and we're in Rome, the most powerful city in the world...and the Gospel is penetrating this great city."

I was happy for what God had done for me and the additional money only reinforced my spirits.

"I must write the Philippians to tell them what a joyful thing it is to serve God…even if I have these chains." I rattled my shackles for everyone in the apartment to hear. They smiled sheepishly.

The next morning, I was on the balcony ready to dictate a letter to the Philippians. I could hear the merchants in the marketplace pleading with women to buy their merchandise. It was early in the morning and women were out shopping for their daily bread.

I began my letter, "Paul and Timothy, servants of Jesus Christ, to all the saints in Philippi with the elders and deacons…"

I leaned back in my chair and smiled about the introduction. I didn't need to remind anyone of my apostolic authority, especially in Philippi. This was a church that loved me and prayed for me. There was no theological heresy in the church to correct, and the only problem was two elderly women who fuss about everything. I'll write that Euodia and Syntyche honor one another. To be rebuked in front of everyone should correct the problem.

The Philippi church had been established on my first trip into Greece. Not only was it a prosperous church, but they readily received and studied the Word of God. The people are grounded in Scripture.

Philippi is a Roman colony, therefore there is a strong presence of law and order in the streets. But there are not many Jews there, so there is no synagogue. I realize that in places like Thessalonica, Ephesus, and Corinth there were contentious Jews who attacked me because there were synagogues in those cities.

Also, in cities where there are synagogues, Judaizers greatly pressure the Christians in these young churches. But that was not true in Philippi.

A street salesman yelled under the balcony, interrupting my thought about the other church. I came back to my writing to the Philippians. I wrote that even though I had chains, the Gospel is preached in Caesar's palace. Also, these chains remind me that four times each day a Roman soldier comes to guard me. That is four opportunities each day to present the Gospel to a soldier. When they accept Jesus Christ as Savior, these soldiers become more than representation of the Roman Empire, they become God's soldiers in the Kingdom of Grace. When their duties transfer them into the palace, they preach Christ. But most importantly, these soldiers have been transferred to places throughout the entire Roman Empire. God is using them to spread the Gospel of Jesus Christ to the ends of the earth. They have helped fulfill the last command of Jesus to the church.

As I continued writing to the Philippians, I couldn't help using the word *joy* and *rejoice*. The beautiful day made me rejoice in Christ. But also the people in Philippi are good people, they are happy in the Lord. Their joyful reputation made it easy to write this letter of hope.

Epaphroditus will deliver this letter to Philippi. I will tell him to instruct the people of Philippi to let those itinerant preachers who come to their town to make copies of this letter to share with other churches.

Sincerely yours in Christ,
The apostle Paul

# PRAYING THE BOOK OF PHILIPPIANS

## Paul's Confidence in Spite of Suffering

### Philippians 1:1-30

Lord, Paul and Timothy considered themselves Your slaves,
    I too will be Your slave, You are my Master.
They wrote to all the saints and church leaders at Philippi
    Greeting them with Your grace and peace.
Paul thanked God for their salvation and godly life;
    In the same way, I am grateful for my salvation
    And I rejoice in opportunities to pray for my family and friends
Because of their partnership in helping me proclaim the Good News
    From the very first until now.

Lord, I know that You who began the good work of salvation
    Will continue it in me until the day You return;
You are always on my mind and in my heart,
    So it is only right that I have this confidence.

Lord, You have given me the privilege of serving You
    Both in difficult circumstances and good days;
This deep assurance comes only from
    Your heart, O Christ Jesus, my Savior.

Lord, I pray that my love of family and friends will keep growing
    And that they will grow in true knowledge
    And perfect understanding of You,
So they will always make the best choices
    And live pure and blameless lives.
I want them filled with all the good qualities

That only You can produce in them;
I pray this for Your glory and praise.

Lord, may my family and friends understand what You
          Have done in my heart
          That makes me share the Gospel with others,
All those about me know that I am Your slave;
          This has given me boldness to serve you
          And to spread Your message without fear.

Lord, I know some preach the message of Christ
          Out of jealousy or competition,
          But others preach out of a pure heart.
They are motivated by Your love
          Because You have given all of us this task.
Still others preach Christ for the wrong motives
          Doing it out of selfish pride.
I don't care what their motives are,
          Just as long as You, Christ, are preached.
Whether You are preached from right or wrong motives,
          I will rejoice and continue rejoicing
Because I know You will use the message
          To set many free.

Lord, it is my earnest desire and hope
          That I will never embarrass You,
But that with all boldness as always
          You will be magnified in my body
          Whether it is by life or death.

Lord, my passion is to live for You, O Christ,
          And if I die, it will be my gain.
If I go on living in this body,
          I will still continue serving You.
So I am not sure which option I want,

I want to leave this body to be with You
Which seems the best choice for me.
But if I stay in this body to serve You,
I can still accomplish much for You.
So, I am sure that if I stay and continue my ministry,
I can further Your work in many believers.

Lord, I pray that my family and friends will continue living for You,
that whether I remain on this earth or die,
they remain firm in their faith in the Gospel.

Lord, I pray they will not be afraid of their enemies,
But be courageous in Your care;
Because the testimony of my family and friends
Will convict their enemies of their sin
And make them aware of perdition.

Lord, You have given all of us the privilege of believing in You,
But also, suffering on Your behalf;
My family and friends are both in the same struggle—
What I fight, they also fight.
Amen.

## Christ, the Pattern for Believers

### Philippians 2:1-30

Lord, I want the same harmony for believers today that Paul wanted for the
Philippians;
Many believers have one purpose in life
Because we all belong to Christ,
And we are encouraged by His love,
And we have fellowship with the Holy Spirit.
You have made our hearts tender and compassionate,

As we have a common purpose to glorify Jesus Christ,
  And to love one another and work together to serve Him.

Lord, help me keep egotistical desires out of the picture,
  And keep me from selfishness.
Help me regard others as better than myself,
  And keep me from thinking only of my agenda.
Help me be interested in others
  And not just my own affairs.

Lord, I want the same attitude toward others,
  As Jesus showed by His example of humility.
Even though Jesus was God
  He did not make exceptions for Himself because of His deity.
On the contrary, Jesus emptied Himself
  And took on human flesh and became a servant.
He humbled Himself even more;
  Jesus became obedient to death
  And died as a criminal on the Cross.
Therefore, You raised Jesus to the highest possible position
  And gave Him a name above every name.
So that at the name of Jesus,
  Every knee will bow in Heaven, earth, and under the earth,
And every tongue will declare that Jesus Christ is Lord,
  To Your glory, O Father.

Lord, Paul reminded the Philippians that they followed his instructions
  when he was with them. Now he wants them to be just as obedient
  while he is away from them, because their reverence and fear
  demonstrates to everyone their salvation.

Lord, give me a deeper desire to serve You, just as You gave the Philippians
  the power to please You.

  *Help me do everything without griping or complaining*
    *So that I have a blameless and faultless testimony to all.*

*Help me live a clean life as Your child*
   *So I'm a light in a dark and lawless world.*

Lord, help me grab tightly to the Word of life
   so that I'll be faithful until Christ returns.

Lord, help me run my race victoriously
   so that my works will not become useless.
   Even if I die a martyr's death like Paul,
   I will rejoice in this opportunity.

Lord, Paul wanted to send Timothy to the Philippians to find out how they
   were getting along. That would encourage Paul. Because Timothy
   was Paul's trusted helper who put other people's interests
   ahead of his own.

Lord, Paul was grateful for Timothy who was like a son to him.
   Timothy also sacrificed with Paul for the Gospel. Paul told them as
   soon as his affairs in Rome were settled, he planned to visit them in
   Philippi.

Lord, Paul also wanted to send Epaphroditus back to the Philippians. He
   had brought money to Paul from them. Paul was concerned
   because the Philippines heard Epaphroditus was sick and had
   almost died. But God had mercy and he lived. Paul said that his
   death would have been an unthinkable burden.

Lord, Paul was eager to send Epaphroditus back to see them because the
   Philippians wanted to see him. "Welcome him with Christian love,"
   Paul said. Epaphroditus had almost died doing for Paul the things
   the Philippians couldn't do for Paul because they were so far away.
                  Amen.

## Christ, the Object of Believers' Desire

### Philippians 3:1-21

Lord, whatever happens in my life—whether good or bad—
> I want to rejoice in Your provision for me,
> just as Paul never got tired of rejoicing in Your provision for him.

Lord, keep me safe from the pressures of mean-spirited legalists
> Who bite at me like a dog.
> They want everyone to keep the Law to be saved.

Lord, I have the true circumcision of the heart and I worship You
> in the Holy Spirit, and I rejoice in Christ Jesus.

Lord, Paul had better qualifications than all the legalists, so Paul could
> have been the best of all strict legalists. But Paul didn't put
> confidence in the flesh, but in Your grace.

Lord, Paul was born a Jew into the tribe of Benjamin, circumcised on the
> eighth day. Paul spoke Hebrew, kept the Law as a Pharisee, and he
> persecuted the church. Everyone considered Paul blameless.

Lord, just as Paul considered the perfections of his legalism was
> unimportant, help me realize the Law is useless to give me intimate
> fellowship with Christ.

Lord, just as Paul gave up everything for Christ, I also count everything loss
> to have an intimate fellowship with Christ.

Yes, Lord, I give up everything for the knowledge of Christ and I no longer
> treasure them because Christ has become my treasure.

Lord, I am now united in Christ, not having my righteousness based on
> legalism, but based on faith to receive Christ's righteousness.

Lord, I want to experience Christ and the power of His resurrection;
> I want to know what it means to suffer with Christ,

And to share spiritually in His death;
>> And eventually be resurrected from the dead.

Lord, I have not yet reached the goal of Christ,
>> But I keep pursuing it,
So I can become the Christ-dominated person
>> For which You originally pursued me.

Lord, I know I have not attained the goal;
>> I do not consider my life perfect,
But, I focus my entire energies on this one thing,
>> I daily forget past accomplishments and failures
>> And look forward to what lies ahead.
I keep giving all my energy to win the prize
>> Of Your upward calling to me in Christ Jesus.

Lord, all spiritual believers should be doing the same thing;
>> But many are not pursuing Christ.
Show them what they should do.
>> Everyone must live at the level they've learned
>> And obey the truth they know.

Lord, help me follow the example of Paul
>> And learn from the pattern he set for all believers.
There are many who live as enemies of Christ;
>> Paul told us about these people.
They are walking toward destruction,
>> Their belly is their god.
They are proud of their sin
>> When they should be ashamed of it;
>> They live for things in this earth.

Lord, I am a citizen of Heaven
>> And I wait for my Savior, Jesus Christ
>> To come to take me there.
Then He will transform my finite body

To be like His glorious body
With the same power He will use
    To conquer everything on earth.
               Amen.

## Christ, the Believers' Strength

### Philippians 4:1-23

Lord, Paul wanted to see his friends in Philippi that he had won to Christ
    because they were the fruit of his work.

Lord, just as Paul prayed for the Philippians to remain loyal
    to You, may I stay true to You in my faith.

Lord, Paul begged Euodia and Syntyche to settle their
    disagreement and have one focus in serving You.
    Then Paul asked the church to work with these women and with
    Clement to spread the Gospel.

Lord, I rejoice gladly in all Your goodness,
    So always keep me filled with Your joy.
Let my gentleness and goodness be evident to all
    Because Christ may come at any moment.

Lord, I won't worry about anything,
    But I'll pray to You about everything,
    And I'll be thankful for all things that happen.
Then, Your peace will guard my heart and mind
    Because the presence of Christ Jesus in my life
    Surpasses anything that I could ever understand.

Lord, I'll constantly meditate on;
    Whatever things are true,
    Whatever things are honorable,

Whatever things are right,
Whatever things are pure,
Whatever things are lovely,
Whatever things contribute to my having a good reputation for You.

Lord, I'll keep doing in my daily life
the things that Paul does in his life,
then You, the God of peace, will be with me.

Lord, Paul was thankful the Philippians had not quit
expressing concern for him and sending money for his ministry.
Paul did not say this to ask for more money,
but to let them know his appreciation.

Lord, I'm like Paul, satisfied with what I have; I have experienced poverty,
and on other occasions, I've had more than enough. I've learned in
everyway and in every place, to be satisfied with what I have,
whether I am full or hungry, whether I have abundance or poverty.

Lord, I can do all things through Christ
Who gives me the help to get it done.

Lord, Paul thanked the Philippians for sharing in his ministry,
reminding them that they were the only ones who sent money in his
early ministry. Even in Thessalonica they sent money more than once.

Lord, Paul reminded them again he was not asking
for more money, but telling them that their gift will bring them
rewards through his ministry he does for Christ. Paul told them he
had no needs because of the gifts they sent by Epaphroditus. It is a
sweet-smelling aroma that pleased God.

Lord, I want You to care for my financial needs,
The same way you took care of Paul,
From your glorious riches in Christ Jesus.

Glory be to You, my God
>My heavenly Father, forever and ever.

Lord, Paul sent greetings to all the Philippians from all the fellow workers
>with him. Then he sent greetings from all the Christians in Rome,
>especially those who had been saved in the emperor's household.

*Lord, I want the grace of the Lord Jesus Christ*
*To rest on me.*
>>Amen.

# Colossians

## THE STORY OF WRITING
## THE BOOK OF COLOSSIANS

Date: A.D. 64 ~ Written from: Rome, Italy ~ Written by: Paul

I was taking a stroll along the Po River with Epaphras, a fellow disciple of Jesus. My ever-present curious Roman guard was listening to every word I said. This Roman guard had shown great interest in Christianity, but had not yet committed his heart to believe in Christ.

The day was chilly and I had wrapped my tunic tighter with a shawl to ward off the biting wind. A hood over my head kept my body heat from escaping.

Epaphras had heard through friends of some of the problems in the church at Colosse. Epaphras was more than just an idle listener, he was extremely concerned about the church in Colosse. Epaphras knew the rich business man Philemon, and had preached in the church that met in Philemon's home. When Epaphras left Colosse to join me in Rome, he left Archippus with the responsibility of preaching the Word each Lord's day.

"There are two problems in the church at Colosse," Epaphras explained to me. "First, a preacher from Alexandria, Egypt, came with a strong emphasis on asceticism. He kept telling the Colossians, "Touch not, taste not, handle not.""

Since the people at Colosse were hard working and disciplined, they listened to the message of self-discipline and took it to heart. I know the heart is committed to fanaticism when it is not tempered by the head. Some people in Colosse had become fanatical in mortification in the body.

There was another problem. Certain Judaic elements in the church wanted everyone to observe the Law and observe Jewish holy days with super-legalistic fervor.

Even as I listened carefully to the things that Epaphras was telling me, I was beginning to form a letter in my mind I could write to the Colossians. I knew Epaphras was the perfect one to take the letter. The people would listen to him because he had been their pastor, and they would receive the letter I planned to write.

I planned to write a letter similar to the one I sent to the church at Ephesus. I wanted them to exchange letters to get the full exposure of truth in each of them.

Epaphras explained to me there was another problem in Colosse, "There was the error of false mysticism," which Epaphras described as Christians embrace philosophical thought. He also explained, "Christians speak so often about angels that they seem to worship angels."

Epaphras explained the problem to me. "These Christians are so proud of their deep mystical thoughts, that they use them when they preach the Gospel and they embrace logic as a foundation for the Gospel."

Epaphras threw up his hands in disgust, "They are proud of learning, they don't hold to Jesus Christ the head of all things and they don't use the Scriptures to gain wisdom."

As I heard Epaphras explain the problems in the church, I began to write a letter to the Colossians including many of the things I had previously said to the Ephesians. The Colossians needed to know they were wealthy in Jesus Christ, so I planned to write a letter showing that Christ is everything.

I whispered a prayer, "Lord, help me write a statement about Jesus Christ that will make the Colossians realize His superiority and His preeminence."

I also decided to write that they have been raised together with Christ and they sit with Christ at the right hand of God, the Father.

Again, I shook my head in disgust over the philosophical leanings of the Colossians. I plan to write, "Let the Word of Christ dwell in you richly as your wisdom. Teach and admonish everyone according to the Scriptures. Let the people sing the great songs of the Old Testament, also singing the new hymns and spiritual songs when they come together to worship."

I wanted the Colossians to be absolutely committed to Christ, so I wrote, "Whatever you do in speech or action, do all wholeheartedly to God." In case they missed it, I repeated myself, "Whatever you do, do it heartedly to the Lord, and not to men."

Paul and Epaphras decided to sit for awhile in the sun. It was then when Paul explained that Epaphras would take this letter to the Colossians. He would also take the runaway slave, Onesimus, and a letter to Philemon asking this wealthy brother to receive back the escaped slave who had been taking care of household chores for Paul. Epaphras would deliver that letter. Also on his way to Colosse, Paul asked Epaphras to stop by Ephesus and deliver the letter to them.

"This is a strategic job," Paul explained to Epaphras, "I pray that God would speed you on your way so we may strengthen the church at Ephesus and Colosse. Also, I want to help reconcile Onesimus with his master, Philemon."

Sincerely yours in Christ,<br>
The apostle Paul

# PRAYING THE BOOK OF COLOSSIANS

## The Prayer for Believers and the Pre-eminence of Christ

### Colossians 1:1-29

Lord, Paul was led by God to write to the Colossian believers using his
     authority as an apostle to remind them of the greatness of
     the indwelling Christ and to warn them of some new doctrinal
     problems springing up among them.

Lord, may You always deal with me in grace
     as Paul prayed for Your grace on the Colossians.
     And may You give me peace that comes from
     You my God and Father, and from the Lord Jesus Christ.

Lord, Paul gave thanks for the Colossian believers
     from the first time he heard about their salvation,
     and for their new expressions of love for all saints.

Lord, use the testimony of my salvation to encourage others,
     Just as you used the testimony of the Colossians
     To bless others.

Lord, I am looking forward to the promise of Heaven;
     This pledge was mine the moment I first believed,
     Just as it guarantees the same hope to others who believe.

Lord, the Gospel is the power that is transforming my life
     And all other lives everywhere.
This good news is given out all over the world,
     Changing lives, just as it transformed the Colossians.

Lord, Paul reminded the Colossians that Epaphras faithfully
      brought the Gospel to them. Now Epaphras was their
      representative helping Paul in Rome. As a matter of fact,
      Epaphras was the one who told Paul about the strengths and
      problems of the new church at Colosse.

Lord, raise up intercessors to pray for me
      As Paul continually prayed for the Colossians.

Lord, I pray for a total understanding of Your will
      And what You want me to do with my life.
I pray for spiritual wisdom to make decisions
      That will honor and please You.
I pray to continually do good things for others,
      For this is Your command to me.
I pray to know You more intimately
      So I can enjoy fellowship with You.
I pray to be strengthened with spiritual power,
      So I can endure with Your patience;
I pray to be filled with joy so I'll always be thankful
      For the spiritual inheritance You've given me.
I praise You for the freeing power of Christ's blood
      That has forgiven me all my sins.
I'm grateful You have rescued me
      From the kingdom of satanic darkness
      And delivered me into the Kingdom of Christ.

## The Pre-eminence of Christ

Christ, I see You as the perfect reflection
      Of the Father who cannot be seen.
Christ, You existed before the Father created all things;
      And Christ, You are supreme over all things.
Christ, You created everything in Heaven and earth;

You created the things we can see,
You created the things we can't see.
Christ, everything has been created by You and for You,
Including kings, kingdoms, rulers, and authorities.
Christ, You existed before all things were created,
Now Your power holds creation together.

Christ, You are the head of the church
Which is Your living spiritual Body.
Christ, You were the first to rise from the dead;
You are first in everything.
Christ, all the fullness of God the Trinity Who
Lives and dwells in You.
Christ, by You, did God the Father reconcile
All the things to Himself.
Christ, by the blood of Your Cross
God the Father in Heaven made peace with everything
In Heaven and on earth.
Christ, You brought me back as a friend
When I was far, far away as Your enemy
By my evil thoughts and sinful actions.
Christ, You brought me into the very presence of the Father
By the sacrifice of Your body on the Cross.
Christ, I now have access to the Father's presence
Because I am standing there in You,
Holy, blameless, and pure.
Christ, I completely believe this truth about You
And I base my faith on it.
Christ, I will not drift away from this assurance
For this Good News that has saved me
Has also been preached all over the world.

Paul was happy to suffer for the believers in Colosse,
>because he identified with Christ's sufferings, and through
>Christ's sufferings others are brought to saving faith.

Paul was given the commission to spread the Gospel to all Gentiles, a
>message that was not known by them in past generations and
>centuries, but now it has been revealed to them that the riches
>and blessings of Christ is for them also.

Christ, I rejoice greatly in the truth,
>That Christ lives in me, my hope of glory.
>I share this message of You with all people
>So that all believers may become perfect in You.
>Christ, I am motivated with serving You
>Because You energize the Father's work within me.
>>Amen.

## Warning Against False Wisdom and Legalism

### Colossians 2:1-23

Lord, Paul interceded for believers in other churches, even though he
>had not seen them.
>Paul prayed the following request for them. This is the same
>that I pray for those I know and for the larger Body of Christ.

Lord, I pray that they may be encouraged,
>And that they experience strong ties of love to one another.
>I pray that they may have a full understanding of how Your mystery
>will work in their lives so they can live confidently for Christ. I pray
>that they may understand the hidden treasures of wisdom that are
>hidden only in Christ.

Lord, may no one deceive me with cunning arguments
That anyone is the wisdom of God;
I know that only Christ is the wisdom of God.

Lord, Paul was happy that the Colossian believers were living as they
should and their faith was steadfastly rooted in Christ.

Lord, may I always continue to obey Christ Jesus, my Lord,
Just as I did when I first believed in Him.
May I be rooted in the faith, and nourished by Christ
so I'll grow strong in my Christian life,
and may I always be thankful for what Christ has done for me.

Lord, Paul warned the Colossians against those who would lead them
astray by human logic or deceitful theories that come from
depraved thinking or evil principles of the world.
Paul reminded them such "teaching" didn't come from Christ.

Lord, Paul reminded the Colossians that Your fullness—the fullness of
the Godhead—lived in Christ's human body, and that only when
a believer was indwelt by Christ, could he experience Your full
understanding and leadership.

*Lord, I yield to Your will and I seek Your wisdom,*
*For only through Your Lordship in my life*
*can I understand Your plan and accomplish*
*Your will for my life.*

Lord, when I came to salvation in Christ,
I was circumcised—set apart—in my heart; this was not a
physical procedure. I was spiritually set apart from satisfying
my sinful nature so that I might please Christ Jesus. I was
identified with Christ's death, when I was spiritually baptized
into Christ; and I was raised with Christ to new life, by the same
power that brought Him from the dead.

Lord, I was dead in my rebellious sins against You,
   being controlled by my sinful nature; but You forgave all my sins.
   You wiped my record clean of all the charges against me,
   and forgave them by nailing them to Christ's cross.
   Now evil powers have no authority over me, because Christ publicly
   triumphed over sin by His victory on the Cross.

Lord, because I am completely forgiven, no one can condemn me
   for what I eat or drink, or for not celebrating holy days or
   Sabbaths. These Old Testament rules were only a shadow of
   coming things; they pointed us to Christ who fulfilled these rules.

Lord, I'll not let anyone cheat me of my relationship with Christ,
   even when they insist on self-denial or worship of angels;
   for they are puffed up by their deceitful insight. They are not united
   with Christ, the head of the Body, for He nourishes all believers
   into a vital union that grows together by Your nourishment.

Lord, since I have died together with Christ to be separated from this
   sinful world, why would I subject myself to worldly regulations,
   claiming "do not taste, touch, or handle"?

   These are merely human rules that mean nothing, even though
   these rules seem "right" because they demand self-denial and
   humility.

   But they never help me triumph over my evil thoughts and desires;
   victory comes only through the Person of Christ.
                      Amen.

## Our Heavenly Union With Christ
## Determines Our Daily Walk

### Colossians 3:1-25

Lord, since I have been raised to new life in Christ,
    I will control my thinking by the principles of Heaven
Where Christ is sitting at Your right hand
    In the seat of honor and influence.
I will think on things in Heaven and
    Not be controlled by things on this earth,
Because I died when Christ died
    And my new life is hidden by You in Christ.
Then when Christ appears to the whole world,
    I will appear with Him in glory.

Lord, I will put to death any sinful desire—
    My sexual lust, filthiness, evil desires,
    And greed which is idolatry.
These are the vices You punish
    In those who are rebellious to You.
I used to be guilty of these things
    When my life was controlled by the world.
But now that I have Christ dwelling in my life,
    I will get rid of anger, rebellious behavior,
    Slander, and filthy language.
I will not lie to anyone, for I have turned away from
    My old nature with its sinful urges.
I have turned to my new nature
    That You continually renew within me,
    As I learn more and more about Christ.

Lord, all new believers in Christ can be controlled by their
    new nature, whether they are a Jew or Gentile,
    whether they are circumcised or not, whether they

are barbarian, civilized, slave, or free.
Christ is the only power that can control a life,
because He lives in all believers.

Lord, since You chose me to live a holy life,
I will clothe myself with mercy, kindness,
Humility, gentleness, and patience.
I recognize that some believers let these sins disrupt their lives
So, I will forgive their trespasses, as You forgave me.

Lord, love is the most important attitude I can put on
Because love makes me one with all other believers.
Also, I want Your peace to control my heart
Because all believers are called to live in peace.

Lord, I want the rich words of Christ to live in my heart
so that I have His wisdom
to teach and correct other believers.

I want to sing palms, hymns, and spiritual songs
to you with a thankful heart.

May everything I say and everything I do
be expressed in the name of the Lord Jesus Christ,
giving thanks to You my heavenly Father.

Lord, wives must submit to their husbands
Because this is what You desire of them.
Husbands must love their wives
And never be mean to them.
Children must always obey their parents,
For this pleases You.
Fathers must not provoke their children to anger,
Because they will become discouraged and give up.
Servants must obey their earthly bosses in everything,

Not just when they are watching,
But do it from the heart to please You.

Lord, I will do everything with my whole heart,
Because I am working to please You, and not men.
Then You will give me an inheritance as a reward,
And those who do wrong will be repaid for their rebellion,
Because You will not let anyone get away with sin.

Amen.

## Earnest Prayer

## Colossians 4:1-18

Lord, masters who direct servants must be kind and fair
Just as You our Master in Heaven treat us.
Lord, I will give myself continually to prayer,
Always remembering to be thankful.
I will pray for Your ministers to have opportunities
To preach the message of Christ
(This is the reason Paul was in chains).
I will pray that ministers preach the Gospel
As clearly as they can.

Lord, I will live a good testimony among non-Christians
And will use every opportunity to share Christ with them.
I will make sure my words are gracious and useful
With the right answer for everyone.

Lord, Paul told the Colossians that Tychicus will tell them how he was
doing. Tychicus had been faithfully serving the Lord with Paul.

Paul also told how he was sending Onesimus back to them in Colosse. Onesimus had recently been saved and now he was a brother in Christ.

Paul gave the Colossians greetings from Aristarchus who is a prisoner with Paul. He also sent greetings from Mark, Barnabas' cousin. Then Paul told his readers to receive Mark when he comes their way. Finally, Paul sent greetings from Justis. He notes they are his Jewish-Christian co-workers.

Paul sent greetings from Epaphrus, who is from Colosse. Epaphrus continually prayed for the Colossians, asking God to make them strong and mature in their Christian faith. Paul reminds them that Epaphrus is a prayer warrior for all believers.

Paul included greetings from Luke the physician, and Demas; then Paul asked that his greetings be passed on to other believers.

Paul asked the Colossians to pass this letter to the church in Laodicea, and that they should read the letter he wrote to them.

Lord, may I always be as faithful to carry out Your work
as Paul faithfully served You.

Paul signed this letter with his own signature, asking people "Remember my chains" and "May the grace of God be with you."
Amen.

# 1 Thessalonians

## The Story of Writing the Book of First Thessalonians

Date: A.D. 54 ∼ Written from: Athens, Greece ∼ Written by: Paul

I have only been in Athens a short time. I was frustrated that the Judaizers had created a riot in Thessalonica; in essence, running me out of the city. I then went to Berea, and the Judaizers followed me there, but the Christians in Berea had a hunger to know the Scriptures. The Christians at Berea were good people. They came with me to Athens to assure my safety.

Then Silas and Timothy arrived in Athens bringing me news of the Christians in Thessalonica. I had only preached in Thessalonica three Sabbaths, but even in that short period of time, I had covered all the foundational doctrines of Christianity. But Silas and Timothy were concerned about doctrinal problems in the church.

I had a tumultuous ministry in Thessalonica, the second city in Greece I visited. I had gone into the synagogue of Thessalonica to reason with them from the Word of God. I had only stayed about a month in Thessalonica, at least I was there for three weekends of ministry from the Scriptures. Many Jews were converted in Thessalonica, including a good number of Greeks.

But the unsaved Jews refused to hear me. When I went into the homes of the leading men and women to teach them the way of God more clearly, the unsaved Jews couldn't stand it. They felt I was teaching a "deplorable sect" because I didn't insist that the Law be kept by new converts.

The unsaved Jews followed me everywhere, attacking me verbally and wanting to debate with me in the marketplace, in the Forum, and in the streets of the city. When the unsaved Jews saw their tactics were not getting anywhere, they turned to a strategy that denied all their Jewish ancestry. They gathered together a group of hooligans—drunks, petty thieves, and rebels. They instigated a riot in the marketplace and accused me of lawless acts. The riot spread through the streets of the city and reached to the Forum.

Since I had been staying in the house of Jason, they surrounded the house and demanded Jason hand me over to them. Fortunately, I was not there at the time. The mob dragged Jason and other Christians to city courts with the accusation, "These men have turned the world upside down and have come here to create a riot."

"What is their crime?" one of the city rulers asked.

"These men say that Jesus is the King, not Caesar." And the rioters began to chant, "These men teach our citizens to break the Roman laws."

The riot continued getting louder so the city rulers demanded that Jason produce a security bond. The magistrate told him, "If this riot breaks out again, we will keep the security bond, and if we have to, we'll take your home."

It was then when the brethren decided that I and Silas would leave the city. No one was in the city streets at night, so they accompanied Silas and me a short way to the city of Berea.

The unsaved Jews chased me to Berea. It was then I came to Athens, the capital city of all of Greece. This is the center of the intellectual world; it is also the center of idolatry in the Greek world. Everywhere I look I see an idol—all types of mythological men and women are worshiped as well as idols portrayed by animals, birds, and fish. If the Gospel can flourish here, it can influence any city in the world.

Silas and Timothy told me, "You must write to the church in Thessalonica, they are gravely concerned about some who died in the last few months. They want to know what will happen to their dead loved ones when Jesus returns to earth."

I told Silas and Timothy I will write them concerning our great hope, that the next great event on God's calendar will be Jesus appearing in the sky for Christians. I will tell them that those who have died will be resurrected first and *caught up* (meaning "rapture") to be with the Lord. Then we who are alive and walking about will instantly follow them to meet the Lord in the air. Then we will ever live with the Lord.

I can have the letter written in two days, I said to Silas and Timothy. "Then you, Timothy, can take this letter to them and encourage them in the faith."

Sincerely yours in Christ,
The apostle Paul

# PRAYING THE BOOK OF FIRST THESSALONIANS

## Characteristics of a Model Church

### 1 Thessalonians 1:1-10

Lord, Paul along with Silas and Timothy, wrote to the church in
Thessalonica, Greece, reminding them that You, our heavenly Father
and the Lord Jesus Christ, founded the church.
Paul prayed grace and peace on the Thessalonians;
I want that grace on my life.

*Lord, I am thankful that I can pray for others,*
*Never forgetting what their faith meant to me,*
*And how their love strengthened me.*
*I look forward to the return of the Lord Jesus Christ,*
*This hope preserves me in difficulties.*

Lord, Paul reminded his readers how the Gospel came to them by his
explanation and by the demonstrated power of the Holy Spirit.
Paul reminded them that his life was a demonstration of the truth of
his preaching, and that they received his message with joy, in spite
of the persecution that came on the young church.

*Lord, may I be an example to all others*
*Just as the believers in Thessalonica were to those in Greece.*
*May I spread the message of the Gospel out to others,*
*Just as the Gospel reached many because of the Thessalonians.*

Lord, everyone was telling Paul of the strong faith of the Thessalonians, how they welcomed the Gospel, and they turned to Christ from idols to serve You, the Living and True God.

*Lord, I look forward to the return of Your Son from Heaven*
*Whom You brought back from the dead.*
*For He is coming back to deliver us*
*From the terrible wrath and tribulation*
*You will pour out on the world in the future.*
Amen.

## Characteristics of a Model Servant

### 1 Thessalonians 2:1-20

Lord, Paul reminded the Thessalonians about his visit to them and how badly he was beaten in Philippi before coming to them. Paul reminds them of his strong ministry in spite of vicious opposition.

Lord, Paul reminded his readers that he didn't use ulterior motives or impure desires, nor was he trying to trick them. Paul preached as a messenger from God who gave them the message of salvation. He did not preach to please people, but to please God (who knows the motives of people). Paul says that he never used flattery to get them to believe, nor did he pretend to be their friends just to get their support. He also didn't preach to build up a reputation or get human praise. Then Paul reminded them he could have asked for money because he is an apostle of Jesus Christ, but he didn't.

*Lord, help me to be gentle among new believers*
*As Paul was unassuming and kind to the Thessalonians.*
*Help me be loving to new Christians,*
*Willing not only to give them the Gospel,*
*But to give them my own soul as well.*
*Help me care for young followers of Christ*

*To feed and protect them*
*As a mother cares for her baby.*

Paul loved the Thessalonians dearly
    Not only giving them the Gospel,
    But his own life also.

Lord, Paul reminded the Thessalonians that he worked with his hands,
    Slaving day and night,
    So he wouldn't be a burden to them.
Paul reminded them that God was his witness,
    That his treatment of them was fair.
He treated them as a father would treat a son,
    Teaching them what is truthful,
Encouraging them to live worthy of their divine calling,
    Inviting them to share in Your Kingdom of glory.

Lord, Paul was thankful that they received his preaching
    Not as though it were human words,
But as though his message was the very Word of God,
    Which it was; Your living power to transform lives.

Lord, Paul reminded the Thessalonians that they are like the churches in
    Judea, in that they suffer from their countrymen, just as the
    Christians in the Holy Land suffered from the Jews, the ones who
    killed the Lord Jesus and the prophets.
    Those who persecute the church are against both the Gentiles and
    God, because they don't want anyone outside the Jews to be saved.
    Their punishment is adding up in God's records, and one day God's
    punishment will fall on them.

Lord, Paul tells the Thessalonians, "I want to see you,
    Even though you are separated from me physically,
    I still have you in my heart.
"I have longed to come see you

But satan has prevented my coming.
"I live to see my young children in Christ,
        You are my joy, my hope, and my reward.
"You will bring me much joy at the coming of Christ
        For when I stand before God for judgment,
        You will be my glory and reward."
                                    Amen.

## Characteristics of a Model Brother

### 1 Thessalonians 3:1-13

Lord, Paul reminds the Thessalonians that when he went to Athens, he sent
        Timothy to minister to them, even though he was left alone at
        Athens. Paul wanted Timothy to keep them strong in the faith and
        prevent anyone from dropping out.

Lord, Paul reminds them that troubles are part of God's plan for the
        believers. He told them when he was with them that some
        persecution would come, as they have recently experienced. Paul
        was so concerned for them that he sent Timothy to find out if the
        Thessalonians were standing firm in their faith. Paul was afraid the
        Tempter would have tripped them up, and his efforts were destroyed.

Lord, Paul was encouraged because Timothy had just returned to bring the
        good news that the Thessalonians were standing firm. Paul also
        learned the Thessalonians wanted to see him. This news gave Paul
        a lot of confidence in his present trials, and that his ministry of
        planting new churches would succeed, even when trials hit new
        churches. Now Paul was ready to really throw himself in ministry
        because of the positive news that the Thessalonians were standing
        true.

*Lord, I cannot thank You enough*
        *For all the joy I have in Your presence,*

*That Your work prospers in spite of trials.*
*I will pray continually for those in trials*
   *That You will supply what is lacking in their faith.*
*Now may You, the Father of our Lord Jesus Christ,*
   *Help me stand in the face of trials.*
*May You make my love grow*
   *And overflow to those suffering persecution.*
*Make my heart strong, blameless, and holy*
   *Before You, the Father of us all.*
*And may I live a guiltless life,*
   *Because the Lord Jesus Christ is returning*
   *With all those saints who are His.*
                              *Amen.*

## The Hope for All Believers

### 1 Thessalonians 4:1-18

Lord, I know the Scriptures teach that I should
   Please You with my daily life.
And that Scriptures command me to live
   As close as possible to the biblical standards.
You want me to be separate from sin,
   And especially keep away from sexual immorality.
You want me to marry in holiness and purity
   And not in sexual lust as do the heathen,
   For this is a sign they know not God.
I will never sin by having sex with another's spouse
   For You have promised to punish this sin.

Lord, You have not called me to be filthy-minded
   But You want me to think pure thoughts.
If anyone rebels against the rule of purity,
   He is not disobeying man's laws,

He is disobeying Your law
>> And rebelling against the Holy Spirit Who indwells him.

Lord, Paul didn't need to tell them to love their brothers,
>> Since You already taught that in Scripture.
My love is growing toward other Christians
>> And I want to love them more in the future.
My goal is to live a quiet life,
>> To work diligently at my task,
>> And do faithfully all I am required to do.
This way I will influence those who are not Christians,
>> And have enough money to live on.

Lord, Paul didn't want the Thessalonians to be ignorant
>> Of what happens to believers when they die.
So they wouldn't grieve like the world
>> Who has no hope beyond the grave.
Since we believe that Jesus died for us
>> And rose again from the dead,
Those who have died and sleep in Jesus
>> Will He bring with Him at His return.
The Bible teaches that we who are alive
>> at His second coming,
Will not be raptured before these in graves,
>> But they will be raptured first.
For the Lord Jesus will come down from Heaven
>> With a shout as loud as an archangel,
>> And as a blast from a trumpet.
Then the dead in Christ will be the first
>> To rise to meet the Lord in the air.
Then we who are alive and remain on earth
>> Will be caught up with them in the clouds,
To meet the Lord Jesus in the air,
>> To ever live with Him.

*Lord, this promise assures me that I'll live with You forever;*
*I want everyone to know about this prospect*
*So they'll face death with courage and hope.*

Amen.

## Characteristics of a Model Life

### 1 Thessalonians 5:1-28

Lord, I don't expect you to give me dates,
    Because You said "no one knows the
    Exact time of Your return to earth."
All I need to know is that
    "The day of the Lord will come unexpectedly
    Like a thief in the night."
When everyone is saying, "We have peace on earth,"
    Sudden disaster will come
Like labor pains on a pregnant woman,
    And no one can hide from it;
    Everyone, everywhere will be punished.
I have known about Jesus' return,
    I am not in the dark about coming judgment.
I will not sleep spiritually
    But I will watch for Jesus' return.
Night is the time when the unsaved sleep and get drunk,
    But I will live in the light and be sober.
I will be protected by the armor of faith,
    And I will nurture my love
    And I will wear the helmet of hope.

*Lord, I know You never meant for believers*
    *To experience the wrath and tribulation that is coming,*
    *You meant to save us though the Lord Jesus Christ.*
*He died for me so that whether*

*I am alive or in the grave,*
*I will be protected by Him and live with Him.*
*So I will be encouraged by this fact*
*And I will encourage others.*

*Lord, I will be considerate of those who minister*
*Among us as teachers in the Lord.*
*I will honor them and obey them,*
*And I'll not fuss with other believers.*

*Lord, I will warn those not working for You,*
*And give courage to those who are frightened,*
*And will give watchcare to the weak,*
*And will be patient with all.*

*Lord, I pray that no one will pay back evil for evil,*
*But will always do good*
*To believers and unbelievers alike.*
*I will rejoice at all times,*
*And I'll pray constantly,*
*I'll give thinks always to You for everything,*
*Because this is what You expect me to do.*
*I'll not suppress the Holy Spirit's*
*Working in my life,*
*But will listen to the preaching of Your Word.*
*I'll not be gullible, but will analyze everything*
*By the Word of God*
*To determine what is true.*
*I'll stay away from every form of evil*
*And anything that tempts me to sin.*

*Lord, may I grow in the abundance of Your peace,*
*Keep my body, soul, and spirit strong and blameless*
*Until You return to receive me.*

*I know You're faithful to all You call*
*To accomplish Your purpose in their lives.*

Lord, Paul ended his letter asking the Thessalonians to pray for him and greet one another with a holy kiss. He wanted this letter read to all Christians. Then Paul prayed, "The grace of our Lord Jesus Christ be with you."

Amen.

# 2 Thessalonians

## THE STORY OF WRITING
## THE BOOK OF SECOND THESSALONIANS

Date: A.D. 54 ∼ Written from: Athens, Greece ∼ Written by: Paul

It was less than a month after Timothy took my first letter to the Thessalonians that I heard back from them that there were other problems in the church. When Timothy returned with news from the Thessalonians, he told me they had received a forged letter from me that had shaken their faith concerning the Second Coming.

Obviously, the letter was meant to destroy the young church. There were unbelieving Jewish spies in the church who saw the positive effects of my first letter. So, they had a second letter written and forged my signature saying that the persecution of Christians in Thessalonica was really the persecution of the tribulation—the great, and terrible day of the Lord. The poison letter claimed the Christians in Thessalonica had missed the rapture.

While Timothy was away, I had gone into the synagogue to debate with the Jews concerning Jesus Christ. There was little response from the Jews for they were absorbed by the secular city around them and didn't have a heart for the Scriptures nor for God.

Every day I had gone into the marketplace to debate with the Greek philosophers. Some were Epicureans who justified their selfish lifestyle of eating and drinking and making merry. There are also Stoics who believe in self-discipline of every aspect of their life. The philosophers called me a "babbler" and the rumor went about the city that I was proclaiming "some strange god."

I had been busy teaching in the city of Athens. The tall hill in the middle of the city called the Acropolis is topped by the Parthenon. This was a temple built to Athena, the primary goddess of the people in Athens. The Parthenon could be seen from every corner of the city and reminded the people constantly of their idol worship.

Finally, they invited me to Mars Hill, a small hill right below the Parthenon where people gathered to debate and discuss religion. It was there on Mars Hill where I preached,

"I see the men of Athens are very religious, and they have idols to every god known to man. However, when I saw the idol to the "unknown God," this is the one that I want to tell you about. This is the God who created the world and everything in it. He is the Lord of Heaven and earth and He does not dwell in the temple like this Parthenon. It is this God in whom we live and move and have our being. God sent His Son to earth to live without sin and died on a cross for our sins. It was then when God raised Him from the dead...."

When these philosophers heard me preach on the resurrection, they mocked me and refused to listen to me. I couldn't continue my sermon.

Shortly after this, Timothy came back from delivering the first letter. So, I sat down to address the Thessalonians a second time, "Paul, Silas, and Timothy, to the church of the Thessalonians in God the Father and the Lord Jesus Christ...."

I told them, "Do not be shaken in your minds or troubled by a letter." I explained that the day of the Lord, which is the tribulation would not come except first there would be a great falling away from the faith by hypocrites and false teachers, then the antichrist would be revealed, who would go into the temple, receiving worship from those he had blinded. The Holy Spirit who restrains sin will be taken out of the world and when the rapture comes there would be a flood of iniquity in the world. I called the work of antichrist, "the mystery of iniquity." Antichrist will come after Christians are raptured with Christ to do lying miracles to deceive everyone in the entire world.

Of course, many in the world will have questions when thousands of believers are raptured out of the world. They would be asking, "What happened to them?" I wrote that God would send the unsaved a strong delusion because of their rebellion, and they would believe the lie told by antichrist. Because antichrist will have an explanation for their disappearance and because of the spiritual blindness of the unsaved; everyone would believe antichrist.

Timothy told me about another problem in the church. A few people were absolutely convinced that Jesus was coming at any moment, so they had quit working and had gone into the mountains to pray and wait His return. Since they were not working, the rest of the Christians were providing food for them. I wrote the church to not feed them, saying, "Those who don't work, shouldn't eat."

Timothy asked me, "How will the Christians in Thessalonica know you've written this letter?" He explained, "If the Thessalonians were deceived by the previous letter, won't they be skeptical of this letter?"

I smiled and said, "I will sign it with my own name. They have my first letter and they can compare the signatures, they will know I've written it."

Sincerely yours in Christ,
The apostle Paul

# PRAYING THE BOOK OF SECOND THESSALONIANS

## Comfort Because They Are Being Persecuted

### 2 Thessalonians 1:1-12

Lord, Paul, Silas, and Timothy sent greetings to the church in
> Thessalonica which
>> belonged to You the Father and the Lord Jesus Christ. They prayed for
>> grace and peace from You and the Lord Jesus Christ.

*Lord, I continually thank You that my faith is growing,*
> *And my love for others is growing.*

*May I have patience and faith,*
> *When I face trials and troubles.*

*My constant determination will demonstrate that*
> *Your care of me is correct*

*And that I am worthy of the Kingdom of God,*
> *For which I am now suffering.*

*Lord, I know You will repay*
> *Those who persecute Your believers,*

*And reward those who are suffering*
> *With the same inner confidence and peace,*

*We'll all receive when Jesus appears*
> *From Heaven with His powerful angels.*

*Lord, I know You will come in flaming fire*
> *To punish those who reject You,*
>> *And refuse to accept the Good News of the Lord Jesus.*

*They will be punished in everlasting hell,*

219

*Forever separated from Your presence,*
*Never to see the glory of Your Kingdom.*

*Lord, thank You that Jesus is coming to be glorified*
*And be seen by His saints,*
*Who are those believing in Him.*

*Lord, I pray continually that I'll be worthy of Your calling,*
*And be the kind of follower You want me to be.*
*Because this way the name of my Lord Jesus Christ*
*Will be glorified*
*When others see the kind of life I live.*
Amen.

## Antichrist and the Coming of Christ

## 2 Thessalonians 2:1-17

Lord, Paul explained to the Thessalonians about the coming of our Lord Jesus Christ and how we will be gathered to Him. He did not want them alarmed by a false prediction, or rumor, or any letters that claimed to come from him. They had heard that the tribulation of the Day of the Lord had already begun. They were confused because they were suffering more persecution then ever before, and thought the tribulation had begun and Christ had come, but they had missed the rapture.

Lord, Paul told them the Tribulation could not being until the man of sin— the antichrist—was revealed and Christians in name only fall away from the faith. The antichrist will oppose everything about God, and exalt himself so that he is worshiped as God, and he will sit in the temple of God claiming that he is God.

Lord, Paul told these things to the Thessalonians while he was there, now he reminds them that the antichrist cannot come until the Holy

Spirit is taken out of the way, because the Spirit holds back a full onslaught of evil in the world. But the One restraining sin—the Holy Spirit—will be removed when believers are raptured.

Lord, Paul told the Thessalonians that the antichrist will be fully revealed after the rapture, but the Lord Jesus Christ will eventually destroy him with the breath of His mouth and with the glorious appearance of His coming.

Lord, Paul reminded them that the antichrist will be satan's representative full of demonic power, and lying tricks. He will deceive all the lost people who don't have spiritual insight because they have already rejected the truth, and have chosen not to believe it. You will send a strong delusion so that they will believe satan's lie. They will all be punished who refused to believe Your truth and who chose willingly to sin.

Lord, I will forever give You thanks
Because You loved me and
Chose me from the beginning to be saved,
And You set me apart to the Holy Spirit and truth.
I thank You for the Good News that came to me,
And I obtained eternal life through the Lord Jesus Christ.
Therefore, I will stand fast and hold on to the message
That Paul delivered to the churches, by word and by letters.

Lord, I pray that my heart will be comforted and
Be established to do every good work,
By You, the heavenly Father, and the Lord Jesus Christ,
Who loves me and gives me the hope of His return.
Amen.

## How To Live While Waiting for Christ's Return

### 2 Thessalonians 3:1-18

*Lord, Paul asked for the Thessalonians to pray for him,*
> *As he prayed for them.*

*I pray that the Word of the Lord*
> *May spread quickly,*
>> *And be effective in winning many to Christ.*

*I ask that I'll be delivered from people*
> *Who are evil and bigoted because they have no faith.*

*Lord, I know You are faithful to give me strength*
> *And will guard me from the evil one.*

*I have believed that Your Word,*
> *Will continue to be successful.*

*May You turn many hearts to Your love*
> *And that they may wait patiently for Christ's return.*

Lord, Paul gave the Thessalonians a command
> To avoid a believer who is lazy
> And avoids work that he should be doing.

Paul wanted his example to be imitated
> Because he was not idle but worked hard
> And paid for his own meals.

Paul worked constantly and he worked diligently
> So he wouldn't be a financial burden on them.

He wanted to be an example for them to follow,
> Even though he had the right to expect a salary.

Lord, Paul gave them a rule when he was there,
> "Don't give food to anyone who refuses to work."

Paul heard that some Christians were lazy,
> Refusing to hold a job,
> And trying to live off those who were working.

Paul ordered them by the authority of the Lord Jesus Christ
To begin working and earning the food they eat.

*Lord, I have learned from Paul and the Thessalonians*
*To never tire of doing the right thing.*
*If any refuse to obey the command of Paul*
*I'll have nothing to do with them,*
*So they'll be convicted of their wrong ways.*
*However, he is not an enemy to Christ;*
*He is a brother who needs correction.*

*Lord, I pray to receive the peace that is Yours,*
*May I receive it in every day, in every way;*
*Lord, be with me!*

Lord, Paul finally greeted all the Thessalonians in his own handwriting; that
gave genuineness to this letter. Finally, Paul prayed for the grace of
the Lord Jesus Christ to be on them.
Amen.

# 1 Timothy

## THE STORY OF WRITING THE BOOK OF FIRST TIMOTHY

Date: A.D. 65 ⌁ Written from: Northern Greece ⌁ Written by: Paul

I felt good to be out of prison. Yet, I constantly rubbed the wounds on my wrists from those four years of chains. These scars are a visible reminder of my prison experience in Caesarea and Rome. While physical freedom felt good, it was nothing like the freedom Jesus Christ gives me from the Jewish Law.

I have had good memories about that second story apartment overlooking the street in Rome. It was there where I wrote some of my greatest letters—letters to Ephesus, Colosse, and Philippi. I wish every church could read those letters to discover and enjoy the riches they have in Christ Jesus.

I feel good about the church in Ephesus. Because it is a church of spiritual riches, they know the Scriptures plus they have experienced revival. They know the power of God. I am glad that Timothy is now preaching in that church.

It was only a few days ago when I received word that there were some problems in Ephesus. These were not problems of outward sin, as was the case in Corinth. There were no doctrinal problems, as was the case in Thessalonica. Nor were there any tendencies to observe Jewish ordinances and holy days, as with the church in Colosse. No...the church at Ephesus is a great testimony because of their love of God and love for one another.

However, there is some tension between young Timothy who pastors the church and the elders of the church. The elders had not been outwardly criticizing Timothy, it's just that Timothy did things differently from they way I did when I was their pastor. I need to write to them to explain some of the differences between different leaders.

And then there's Timothy's side of the story, the elders in Ephesus do things differently from the way Timothy experienced when he pastored the church at Philippi and Berea.

I will write a letter to Timothy to describe how a pastor and elders should relate to one another.

As I picked up a pen to write to Timothy, I thought to remind him that he is my son in the faith. I will remind Timothy that he is a pastor by God's command. I will pray grace, mercy, and peace for Timothy from God the Father and from Jesus Christ.

I will remind Timothy that he must stay in Ephesus to stop certain false teachers from spreading false doctrine. They must stop basing their message on myths and genealogies that create controversy in the church; rather they must build up one another in the Word.

Then I realized, *"The problem with Timothy is that he thinks he is too young for this church."* Even so, I must realize that the church in Ephesus has had great preaching; Apollos, the golden-tongued orator from Alexander. They've also had John, the beloved disciple who leaned on the breast of Jesus. Also, *"they've had me as a preacher."* Then I realized, *"It would be hard for anyone to follow this lineup of preachers, so I have to put myself in Timothy's shoes and advise him accordingly."*

One of the first things I want to write Timothy is, "Let no man despise your youth." I will remind Timothy that even though he is a young man, his authority in ministry is not based on his experience; but, his authority is based on Scripture and God Himself.

And then I know some outward weaknesses of Timothy. He is spending too much time on developing bodily strength and physical exercise, so I'll write to him, "Bodily exercise profits little." But at the same time Timothy's stomach ulcer prohibits him from doing everything he ought to do. So I'll write, "Take a little wine for your stomach's sake." I think I'll underline the world *little* because wine can lead to intoxication. But I know Timothy has good self-control, so I'll not do that.

In Ephesus I hear some of the elders were pushing their friends to become elders. I hear some of the new candidates do not measure up to the qualifications for elders. So I'll write, "If a man desires the office of elder, he desires a good thing...." And then I'll add the set of standards for both elders and deacons in the Ephesus church.

There are also questions about what women could do in the church. Of course in the synagogue, women don't even sit on the main floor with the elders and men of the congregation. Women sit in the loft with the children. I wrote to the Christians at Colosse, "In Jesus Christ, there is no male or female...." Now I'll have to spell out what women should and should not do. This is very touchy because I don't want to exclude women from ministry, but I don't want to go to the other extreme and let them take over authority in the church.

> *If women had not done what women have done,*
> *Where would the church be?*
> *If men would have done what men should have done,*
> *Where could the church be?*

Apparently, some of the elders in the church at Ephesus were not looking after Timothy's financial needs. So I'll write, "Let the elders who rule well be counted worthy of double honor, especially those who labor in the word and doctrine." When I dot the "i" on that sentence, I'll smile because I know the elders won't pay a pastor double salary, they'll just realize Timothy is *worth* a double salary.

Money seemed to be a problem in the church at Ephesus. Not their lack of money, probably, they had *too* much money and didn't use it properly. So I'll remind the church, "The love of money is a root of all kinds of evil." Then I'll outline various principles about how money should be used in the service of the church and for the glory of God.

I'll have a courier take this letter to Timothy as soon as it's finished. I'll sign my name so Timothy will know it's from me. Then copies can be made and sent to every church so pastors and elders will serve God harmoniously.

Sincerely yours in Christ,
The apostle Paul

# PRAYING THE BOOK OF FIRST TIMOTHY

## Paul's Relationship to Timothy and Warning About Heresy

### 1 Timothy 1:1-20

Lord, Paul wrote to Timothy, his son in the faith, reminding Timothy that
Paul was an apostle by Your command and that the Lord Jesus
Christ was his Savior and hope. Paul prays grace, mercy, and peace
for Timothy from You, the Father and from Jesus Christ.

Lord, Paul reminded Timothy that he was to stay in Ephesus to stop certain
false teachers from spreading false doctrine, and to stop the spread
of myths and genealogies that create controversy in the church.
Rather Timothy should build up Your work.

Lord, I know that love comes from a sincere heart,
A pure conscience, and believing faith.
Some have drifted from these qualities
And spend their time arguing about nothing;
So they don't know what they're saying.
I know the Law is good
When we apply it properly to our lives.
I also know the Law is not given to keep
Good people in line,
But the Law is aimed at rebellious people
To teach them the truth,
And point them to salvation.
The Law is aimed at murderers and
Adulterers, and perverts, and slave traders,
And liars, and perjurers.
The Law was written for those who

Deny the Gospel and sound doctrine
And the truth that was committed to Paul.

Lord, I thank You for giving me strength to serve You
And You found me faithful
So that you called me into Your service.
Before I was saved, I was a liar and curser,
And I was against the faith;
I did all this in ignorance.
You showed me mercy,
So that I became a believer.
Your grace filled me with faith
And with love that comes from Jesus Christ.

Lord, this is a faithful saying,
That no one can deny,
Christ Jesus came into the world to save sinners
And I myself was the greatest of them.
Your mercy was shown to me,
Because Jesus Christ meant to make me
A great example of His inexhaustible patience.
As a result, other people have come to trust Jesus
And gain eternal life.

*Lord, I give glory and honor to You, the only God;*
*You are immortal and invisible, forever and ever. Amen.*

Lord, again Paul reminded Timothy, his son,
To do these things he is telling him.
These are the truths spoken by prophets,
So he should fight for them like a good soldier.
His weapons are faith, a pure conscience;
Because some have denied their conscience
They have wrecked their faith.
Such are Hymenaeus and Alexander who are enemies,

Thus Paul has given them to satan to punish them
So they won't bring shame on the name of Christ.
Amen.

## Instructions About Prayer and the Role of Women in Church

### 1 Timothy 2:1-15

Lord, Paul directed Timothy to pray
In every way for all types of people.
I will pray for all people,
Interceding for Your mercy in their lives,
I will give thanks for Your work
In every area of people's lives.
I will pray for political leaders and government supervisors,
So I can live peaceably
And follow holiness and honesty in my life.
In this way, I fulfill my prayer obligation
And will please You, my God and Savior.

Lord, I know you want everyone saved
And learn the full scope of biblical truth.
You are the only God and Christ Jesus—the Man—is the only Mediator
Between You and all people
Because Jesus sacrificed Himself as a ransom
For all the people in the world;
This is the message of truth everyone must hear and believe.
Lord, You appointed Paul as a preacher and apostle,
No one can deny this,
Paul was appointed to teach faith and truth to all.

Lord, because of the way You changed Paul and me
　　　　I will lift freely my hands in prayer to You,
　　　　Free from anger or jealousy.

Lord, Paul wanted women to dress modestly,
　　　　Without being indecent or
　　　　Calling undue attention to themselves,
Paul wanted Christian women to be noticed
　　　　For their inner godly personality
　　　　Not for their outward dress or fixing their hair,
　　　　Or gaudy jewels, or indiscreet clothing.
Paul wanted women to do good works and
　　　　Listen to good Christian women so they could be godly.
Paul didn't want women teaching men
　　　　So that they were in authority over men,
　　　　He wanted them to quietly listen in church.
Paul used the illustration of Adam being created before Eve
　　　　So You created men to be leaders.
But Eve was blinded and deceived by satan,
　　　　Then Adam sinned with his eyes wide open;
　　　　Thus he was guilty and plunged the race into sin.
And women were punished with pain and suffering
　　　　In giving birth to children.
But they will be saved by trusting Jesus the Savior
　　　　And then living quiet lives before You.
　　　　　　　　Amen.


## Qualifications for Pastors and Deacons

### 1 Timothy 3:1-16

Lord, Paul said any man who wants to be a pastor/leader,
　　　　Wants to do a noble work for You.
But he must be a good man; blameless,

The husband of one wife.
He must be self-disciplined, work hard, and obedient;
　　Also, he must be courteous, a good teacher,
　　And open his home to visitors and guests.
A pastor can't drink alcohol, be hot-tempered,
　　But be courteous with people and gentle.
He must not be greedy for money, but must
　　Manage his family well.
Because if a man can't make his family behave,
　　He shouldn't be responsible for church behavior.
A pastor must not be a new convert,
　　Because he may become proud and arrogant.
Then God would condemn him,
　　As God condemned satan for his pride.

Lord, Paul said deacons should live by the same standard
　　As the pastor of the church.
They should be respected by the church
　　And do what they promise.
Deacons should not drink alcohol,
　　Or be greedy for money.
They must be conscientious Christians
　　Believing and walking in faith.
The church must examine them before
　　Putting them into the office of deacon.

Deacons should be the husband of one wife,
　　With happy obedient families.
Those who do a good job as deacons,
　　Should be respected by all in the church.
God will reward them with His blessings,
　　For their faithful walk in Christ Jesus.
In the same way, the wives of pastors and deacons

Must be respectable, not gossipers,
But faithful in every area of life.

Lord, Paul told Timothy he wanted to be with him soon,
But in case he was delayed,
Paul wanted Timothy to know how people should behave
In God's family—the church of the living God—
Because it teaches and protects the truth of God.
Paul gave Timothy the doctrinal statement
For all of the church to learn and believe.

Jesus appeared in a human body,
He was anointed by the Holy Spirit,
Seen by angels,
Preached among the Gentiles,
Believed by many in the world,
And taken up into glory.

Amen.

## How a Good Minister Should Live

### 1 Timothy 4:1-16

Lord, Your Holy Spirit told us that in the last days
Some will turn away from Christ.
They will follow seductive spirits
And will believe false doctrine that comes from demons.
These false teachers will lie about the truth,
They are hypocrites whose consciences are seared
As though they were branded with a red-hot iron.
They will forbid marriage
And demand that people abstain from food.

Lord, You've created every good food to eat,
And I should reject no food

But we must thankfully enjoy it all.
Provided I've blessed it and given thanks,
    Your Scripture and prayer make it holy.
Paul told Timothy to explain this to the church,
    As a good pastor who knows the Word of God.
Paul also told him not to waste time
    Arguing with those deceived by
    Godless myths and old wives tales.
Paul told Timothy to develop his spirituality;
    I also will follow this advice.

Lord, Paul told Timothy physical exercise is all right,
    But don't go to extremes with it.
Spiritual exercise is unlimited,
    It rewards us with a good life here on earth
    And will reward us in Heaven.

Lord, I will give myself diligently to ministry
    And will take whatever suffering comes,
    So that people will believe in Christ.

Because I believe Christ died for me and lives forever,
    My hope is in Him, along with all who put their trust in You.
Help me teach these things to everyone,
    And let no one ignore me because of my age.
Help me be an example to all believers,
    In my speech, behavior, love, faith, and purity.
Help me discipline my time by reading
    The Word of God to people,
    Then preaching and teaching it to them.
I will use the spiritual gifts You gave me,
    That came to me through the Scriptures
    And have been recognized by the church.
I will put all my energy into my work,
    I want everyone to see what You are doing through me.

Therefore, I will be careful of what I do and teach
    So that people will be saved who hear me,
And I will fulfill Your calling for my life.
    Amen.

## The Good Work of a Minister

### 1 Timothy 5:1:25

Lord, You told me never to speak harshly to elderly men,
    But to speak to them respectfully as to a father.
You told me to speak lovingly to younger people
    As I would speak to those in my family.
You told me to treat elderly women
    As I would treat my own mother.

Lord, You have instructed the church to take care of widows
    If they don't have anyone else to care for them.
Their children or grandchildren are the ones
    Who should take responsibility for them
To repay the debt they owe to their elders
    For a grateful heart pleases You very much.
But the church should especially care for widows
    When they have no one in this world to care for them.
Then let them spend their nights and days in prayer,
    Nor running around looking for pleasure and entertainment.

Lord, Paul gave Timothy the church principles
    To care for people and do what is right.
The ones who won't care for their needy relatives,
    Especially those in their immediate family,
Have no right to call themselves Christians;
    They are worse than non-believers.
Widows should be involved as a special church worker

When she is 60 years old,
    Having been the wife of one husband.
She must have been hospitable to others
    And helped those in trouble.

The church is not to accept young widows,
    Because they will want to get married again.
And people will condemn them for not keeping their promise
    To be a special committed church worker.
Besides, young widows can become lazy,
    Going from house to house gossiping
    And meddling in others' affairs.
Paul thought young widows should re-marry,
    Have children and look after a home,
    Then no one can accuse them of anything.
Some young widows have already turned from Christ,
    Having been led astray to follow satan.
The relatives of a widow must take care of her,
    And not expect the church to do it.
Then the church can use its money
    To care for needy widows
    Who fit the qualifications of genuine widows.

Lord, Paul taught the church to give worthy pastors
    Double consideration in paying them,
    Especially those who preach and teach well.
The Scripture says, "Never put a muzzle on the ox
    To keep them from eating.
When they work to bring in the crop,
    Let them eat as they work in the fields."
In another place the Scriptures teach,
    "Those who work deserve their pay."

Lord, Paul taught the church not to listen to complaints
    Against the church leaders,

Unless there are two or three witnesses.
If the church leaders are wrong,
    Rebuke them in front of the church
    As a warning to all believers.
Paul said before God, the Lord Jesus Christ, and the holy angels
    To rebuke sinning pastors impartially,
    Whether they are friends or not.
Treat all people equally without favoritism,
    For we are all equal in Christ.

Lord, Paul taught never to choose a pastor too quickly,
    Because some faults may be overlooked.
Therefore, I will learn from the example of my leaders
    To keep myself pure from all sin.

Lord, Paul told Timothy to quit drinking only water,
    But to take some grape juice for digestion
    Because he was frequently sick.

Lord, some people's sins are obvious to all,
    Long before a formal complaint is made against them.
Others have sins that are not easily discovered
    Until they actually come to light.
In other cases, the sins of some
    Will not be discovered until Judgment Day.
The same truth applies to the good deeds that some do,
    They will not be hidden forever.
        Amen.

## Warnings to a Minister

### 1 Timothy 6:1-21

Lord, workers should work hard for their bosses,
    And respect them in all ways.

May Your name and Christian expectations
      Not be laughed at by the world
      Because Christians are lazy workers.
A worker must not take advantage of his boss
      Because he is a Christian.
On the contrary, Christian workers must do better
      Since they are helping their boss
      To make their business effective and successful.
Paul told Timothy to teach these principles
      And those who have a different interpretation
      Are both selfish and ignorant
Because these truths are biblical and effective,
      Based on the words of the Lord Jesus Christ.
Those who question these truths stir up arguments,
      That lead to anger and jealousy and abuse;
      They do it to make a profit from religion.

Lord, Paul told us we are truly rich
      When we are happy and satisfied with what You give.
We have brought nothing into this world
      And we will take away nothing when we die.
So, as long as we have food and clothing,
      We should be content.
Those who are passionate about being rich,
      Are open to all types of temptations
      And get-rich-quickly schemes.
Their financial lust will hurt their walk with Christ
      And eventually destroy their life,
Because the love of money opens people up
      To all kinds of sin.
Those who spend their life chasing wealth,
      Have wandered away from Your standards for living
      And opened up their souls to fatal wounds.

Lord, because I am dedicated to You,
> I will avoid the evils associated with money.

I purpose to live a saintly life
> And I will seek to be filled with faith, love, and gentleness.

I will fight to put You first in all my life,
> I will hold tightly to eternal life that You give.

This is my calling and my commitment,
> And I have confessed this to the church.

Now before You—the source of life—and before Jesus Christ,
> I promised to do all that I say I will do,

So that no one can find any fault in me
> Both now and in the future till Christ returns.


Paul told Timothy to warn those who are rich in this world
> That they don't look down on others,
> Or trust in their money,

But trust in God, who out of His riches
> Gives us all we need to be happy.

Timothy was instructed to tell rich people
> To use their money to do good.

They are to be rich in good works,
> Generous and willing to share with those in need.

This way rich people can store up real wealth
> For themselves in Heaven;
> This is the only safe investment in life.

Paul told Timothy to guard carefully the commission
> That God had entrusted him.

Keep out of pointless arguments
> Of those who show off their knowledge
> Because they are not really that smart.

They have missed the most important thing in life,
> They don't know You at all;
> May they continually experience Your grace.

Lord, I believe the teaching of Scripture that states;
>    Christ will come soon to rapture His believers,
Christ is blessed by You, and He is the only ruler of all things.
>    He is the King of Kings, and Lord of Lords.
Christ alone is immortal, He is eternal;
>    He now lives in light so pure and blinding
>    That no one can approach Him,
>    No natural person has seen Him.
Now, unto Christ be honor, power, and eternal rulership,
>    For ever and ever; Amen!
>>    Amen.

# 2 Timothy

## THE STORY OF WRITING SECOND TIMOTHY[1]

Date: A.D. 66 ⌁ Written from: Rome, Italy ⌁ Written by: Paul

I knew both sounds clearly. The heavy *clanking* sound—like the dropping of heavy metal bars—is the sound of the gate with steel bars at the end of the hall. The large iron bars are so big that even the strongest of men couldn't bend them. If every evil man in this jail put his weight against that iron door, it wouldn't budge.

Then there is a second sound, the heavy *thud* of the door to my cell. It sounds like a wooden bench dropping on a stone floor. When slammed, the heavy door has a finality of distant thunder. The room is then pitched into darkness. And this hole in the ground called a jail cell is cold—frigid like a wintery night.

With every *clang* of the outer door, my heart jumps. I can't see but I want to know who's there. I listen for a voice, the lonely cell seems more isolated when all my friends are gone.

My heart keeps looking for an escape from this cold, damp prison. With every *clang*, I expect a message of pardon from the Caesar or one of my faithful friends bringing me a warm coat...or books to read...or good news from one of the churches.

But no one comes to see me. Each *clang* is like another nail in the coffin...nothing!

This morning I woke up with a phrase on my mind that I had written to the Philippians, "For me to live is Christ...but to die is gain." Yes, it is hard to live in this damp hole in the ground, but it's easy when Christ dwells in my heart. Sometimes a breeze finds its way down the staircase through the iron bars. I wonder if I'll feel its freshness today.

The worst part of being in isolation is there's nothing to do, nothing to read, there's just nothing…but my thoughts, and they're good thoughts. Just think of all God has allowed me to do.

This morning as I prayed for all of my helpers, I was encouraged by their freedom and what they could do for Christ. Each time I prayed for Barnabas…or for Titus…or for Sosthenes…I got vicarious strength from what they could do for God.

Today I prayed again for Demas, a young man with great potential…I thought that I must tell Timothy about Demas, I will write, "Demas has forsaken me for present worldly attractions." The thought of those pleasures making Demas happy took the air out of my sails. How can I pray for Demas who at one time prayed so zealously? How could I pray for Demas' prosperity when I remember the great sermon he preached from the Scriptures? *"Yes,"* I thought, *"Demas has forsaken me because he loves the pleasures of this world."* I squeezed my eyes to shut out the pain.

I thought I would write to Timothy, "Come to me quickly." I want Timothy here if I should die. I can trust Timothy to tell everyone my last thoughts and words.

And then I thought, *"I'll ask Timothy to bring the books for me to read…"* And as I shiver in this cold, I'll add, *"Bring my cloak."*

The afternoon sun didn't reach my prison cell till after lunch—if you call those starvation rations lunch. I hadn't sat in the warming rays of the sun for two weeks. I know when the afternoons came because the sun filters through the iron bars for about an hour. However, the last two weeks have been cloudy. "Lord, I need sun today." As soon as I prayed, the prison got a little lighter—light enough for me to see with my infected eyes—light enough for me to write a few large letters.

I told myself, *"Rush to take advantage of the sunlight,"* I sat at a feeble table, squeezed the feather into the small bowl of ink, and began to scratch on the pages. "Paul, an apostle of Jesus Christ by the will of God…" It never crossed my mind that prison was a mistake, I knew God had ordained chains for me and shortly I would die. I thought, *"I must include the phrase—'I am now ready to be offered as a sacrifice to God, and I am ready to become a martyr, my departure from this life is at hand.'*

I didn't want this letter to be too gruesome, I didn't want to discourage Timothy.

I smell some smoke drifting through my cell, so I realize the guard was also cold. The guard was stirring the black ashes in the small fire at the end of the hall. As the guard blew on the black ashes, the embers turned red with fire, and a few seconds later, a flame jumps from the midst of the coals. *"I'll write that…"*

I'll write for Timothy to *"stir up the gift of God as one stirs up a fire."* Paul remembers that Timothy is meek and quite often needs his fires stoked. Timothy needs to feed the fire again.

Timothy has a very prestigious position. He is now the preacher of the church in Ephesus, the largest city in Turkey, the Roman capital of Asia Minor. The church at Ephesus includes the wealthy, as well as the extremely poor. In my mind, the church at Ephesus is one of the most important churches for the continuation of the Gospel and Timothy has the awesome responsibility of leading this church of Ephesus.

So I'll write to Timothy, "Be strong in the grace that is in Christ Jesus," reminding Timothy not to bow to the pressures of politicians, rich men or those with great family inheritance. "Rather," I'll write, "endure hardness as a good soldier of Jesus Christ." I want to remind Timothy that a soldier obeys only his commander, no one else. And so, I want Timothy to obey only the Lord Jesus Christ, not elders, not other itinerant preachers, no one else but Jesus.

Then I thought again about the youthful lusts that had enticed Demas, so I write to Timothy, "Flee youthful lust and follow righteousness." This is my deepest prayer for my young preacher in Ephesus.

Day after day I add to the letter that would be sent to Timothy. I write slowly because of weak eyes, I write until it becomes too dark to see the paper. No one provides me with even the smallest candle. When the sun goes down outside, the prison hole in the ground becomes night.

Each night I fluff what is left of the straw on the stone ledge where I sleep. Even in sleep the hard cold stone punishes my flesh. After prayers, I turn on my side to sleep. I dream of being led outside the main gate called the People's Gate to the city of Rome. It's there I'll probably die.

When the soldiers led me into the city, I had seen the crosses on both sides of the road, stretching over the horizon. On each cross was a martyr whose life was "hid in God" because they had given everything for Christ. I wondered if I would be crucified, and if so, "*I am crucified with Christ, nevertheless, I live. But it is not I who will live or die, it is Christ who lives in me.*"

Later my dream turns to the sharp end of a sword. I remember James the fisherman from Capernaum, the brother of the apostle John. His head was cut off by Herod. I wonder if there was a sword in my future. I had written earlier to the Galatians, "*I die daily.*" One day I will die and that will be the last time I die and then I'll receive eternal life.

I had heard the stories of Christians being hung on a tall spike in Nero's garden. I heard the stories of oil being poured on them and their bodies burned to illuminate the parties of the insane Caesar, Nero. "*Will that be my end?*" I wondered. Then I smile, "*What better way to end my life after I've been ablaze for God all over the world?*"

I have one more thought, "*It doesn't make any difference how I die, because I've written, 'To be absent from the body is to be present with the Lord.' So it's much better to die and be with the Lord, than it is to remain in this life.*"

Before going to sleep, I pray, "*Lord, may I glorify You in my death as I have in my life.*"

And right before sleep coverers my mind, I think, "*Maybe Jesus Christ will come with the dawn, which would be nice.*" So my last prayer before going to sleep, "*Even so come, Lord Jesus.*"

Sincerely yours in Christ,
The apostle Paul

# Endnote

1. Paul's second imprisonment in Rome.

# PRAYING THE BOOK OF SECOND TIMOTHY

## Paul's Charge to Timothy

### 2 Timothy 1:1-18

Lord, Paul told Timothy he was appointed by Jesus Christ to be an apostle
>    to tell everyone that eternal life is promised to those who believe.
Timothy was a son to Paul in the faith;
>    Paul prayed for Timothy to have grace, mercy, and peace
>    From You the Father, and from Christ Jesus, our Lord.

Lord, Paul remembered Timothy in prayer night and day
>    And he longed to see him,
>    Because Timothy cried when they left each other.
Paul remembered Timothy's genuine faith
>    Which was first in his grandmother Lois,
>    And in his mother Eunice.
Paul said to stir up the inner fire You gave Timothy,
>    Which was evident at his ordination
>    When Paul laid hands on him.

Lord, You have not given me a spirit of cowardice
>    But a spirit of power, love, and self-control.
So, I will never be ashamed of witnessing for Christ,
>    Or ashamed of other Christians.
I will accept my share of hardships as I share the Gospel,
>    Relying on Your power to accomplish Your will.

Lord, You have saved me and called me to holiness,
>    Not because of anything I've done
>    But for Your purpose and by Your grace.

Your kindness and love was shed on me
  Before the beginning of the world,
But was revealed when our Savior, Christ Jesus,
  Abolished sin and proclaimed life by His death;
  Lord, I believed it and received it.

Lord, Paul again reminded Timothy he was a preacher
  And because he was an apostle to the Gentiles,
  He is also suffering hardships.

Lord, I am not ashamed of the Gospel
  Because I know I've put my trust in Christ.
And I have no doubt You, Father, are able to care
  For all I've entrusted to You until that Day
  When Jesus Christ will return to earth for me.

Lord, I will continue to believe and live
  By the sound teaching I've learned from Scripture.
I will guard Your special calling for my life
  By the help of the Holy Spirit who lives in me.

Lord, Paul reminded Timothy that Phygellus and Hermogenes
  Have refused to have anything to do with Paul.
Paul prayed blessings on Onesiphorus' home
  Because he was not ashamed of Paul's chains.
Onesiphorus came to see Paul in jail
  And helped him when he was in Ephesus.
Onesiphorus went to a lot of trouble to find Paul
  When he was in Rome.
Paul prayed a blessing on him,
  Knowing he would be rewarded at the Judgment Seat of Christ.
    Amen.

## How to Minister in the Day of Apostasy

### 2 Timothy 2:1-26

Lord, I will be strong in the grace
    That comes from Jesus Christ.
All the truth I heard from my teachers,
    I will communicate to trustworthy people
    Who in turn, will be able to teach others.
I will take my share of difficulties
    As a good soldier of Christ Jesus.
No soldier gets bound up with worldly things
    Because he must always obey his commanding officer;
    Therefore, I will separate myself from sinful things.
An athlete cannot win a contest
    Unless he keeps all the rules;
    Therefore, I will discipline myself to obey Christ.
And a farmer gets first claim on the harvest
    Over any crops growing in his field;
    So, I will work hard to get Your reward.

Lord, I will remember the Gospel of Jesus Christ;
    He was a descendent of David,
    He died for me and was raised from the dead.
This is the Gospel for which Paul was being persecuted;
    Paul was chained like a criminal,
    But Your Gospel is not chained.
Paul suffered all his persecutions for the sake
    Of those who have believed the Gospel,
That they may be saved by Jesus Christ and obtain
    Eternal glory that comes to those who are saved.

Lord, Paul gave Timothy a faithful saying
    That he could rely on and share with others.
If I have died with Christ on the Cross,

I will live with Him in Heaven.
If I hold firm in my profession of faith,
      I will reign with Him in glory.
If I deny Christ, He will deny me;
      If I become faithless, Christ is always faithful.

Lord, Paul told Timothy to remind the church about this truth
      And not argue with anyone over this statement of faith,
      Because it will only destroy those who are listening.
I will study to know everything about Christianity,
      So I can be Your approved workman.
I will not be ashamed of my ministry,
      But will rightly handle the word of truth.
I will avoid foolish discussions
      Which make people get angry and sin against one another,
      As it destroyed Humenaeus and Philetus.
They claimed the resurrection of the dead had passed,
      Departing from the truth of God; then
      They dragged others down with their self-destruction.

Lord, even though there are false teachers,
      I know Your truth is as solid as a rock.
You know all who belong to You,
      And all who call on Your name,
      Must avoid doing wrong things.

Lord, in a large home there are all kinds of dishes,
      Some are made of gold and silver, others of wood and clay.
Some dishes are used for special people,
      Other dishes are used for ordinary things.
I want to be a special dish used by my Master, Jesus Christ,
      And kept ready for His good work.
Instead of giving into the lust of youth,
      I will seek holiness, faith, love, and peace
      In fellowship with all who call on the Lord.

I will avoid foolish arguments which upset people,
    And lead to quarrels.
So, I will not quarrel with anyone, but will be kind,
    A good teacher and patient with all.
I will be gentle when I correct people who disagree with me,
    Remembering You can change their mind;
So that they will recognize the truth,
    And escape satan's grip on them,
    And be free of his trap.
        Amen.

## The Prediction of Apostasy and God's Answer in Scripture

### 2 Timothy 3:1-17

Lord, I know that in the last days before Christ comes,
    There will be dangerous times.
People will be aggressively self-centered and greedy for money,
    Boastful, arrogant, and scoff at You.
They will be contentious and ungrateful to their parents,
    And lack any sensitivity for people.
They will be inhumane, without love and without forgiveness;
    Plus they will be sarcastic, violent, and rebellious.
They will hate anything good, but they will be treacherous,
    Rash, conceited, and addicted to pleasure,
    Rather than lovers of God.
They will say they're a Christian and attend church,
    But their life will deny what they profess.
I won't have anything to do with these people,
    I'll keep away from them.

Lord, these types of people break up homes,
    Having sex with stupid people who are obsessed with sex,
    Trying one fantasy after another.

They continually try to educate themselves,
>     But they never come to the truth.
Men like this defy the truth just as Jannes and Jambres defied Moses,
>     They have polluted minds and
>     They have turned against the Christian faith.
And in the long run they won't be very influential;
>     Their folly will be their downfall,
>     And everyone will see their rebellion.

Lord, I know that Paul taught that we who believe in God
>     Should also live godly lives.
Just as Paul demonstrated faith, patience, and love
>     In a consistent life-long way,
Paul was persecuted in Antioch, Iconium and Lystra,
>     But You Lord, rescued him from all of them.
Therefore, anyone who tries to live a life
>     Dedicated to Christ will be attacked.
These wicked imposters of Christianity
>     Will go from bad to worse,
>     Deceiving themselves as they deceive others.

Lord, I will be true to the teachings of Scripture,
>     Remembering who my teachers were and what they taught me,
Just as Timothy remembered his teachers from childhood,
>     Making him wise in the Scriptures
>     So that he accepted Christ and was saved.
The whole Bible was written by Your inspiration,
>     And is useful to teach me the truth,
And points out what is wrong in my life,
>     Helping me to do what is right.
The Bible is Your tool to prepare me
>     In every area of my life,
>     So I can do Your work.
>
> Amen.

## Paul, a Faith Servant

### 2 Timothy 4:1-22

Lord, Paul reminded Timothy that he stood before You
    And before Christ Jesus, who will judge the living and the dead
    At His appearing when He sets up His Kingdom.
I will preach Your Word continually,
    At every place, at all times,
    When it is suitable and when it is not.
I will correct all false teaching and rebuke
    Those who believe and spread it around.
I will encourage all people to do the right thing all the time,
    Based on what Your Word teaches.

Lord, the time is coming when people won't listen to the truth,
    But will seek out teachers who reinforce their sin.
They won't listen to Your Word,
    But will live by their misguided rebellious ways.
I will be careful to always follow Your principles,
    I will always be ready to suffer for Christ.
I will try to win others to Christ,
    And do the things I should do.

Lord, Paul testified it was time for him to die,
    His life was being poured out
    As a sacrifice to You.
Paul said, "I have fought a good fight to the end,
    I have run the race to the finish line,
    I have kept true to the faith."
Now Paul expects the crown of righteousness
    That You have for faithful witnesses
    That will be given to all who look for Christ's' appearing.

Lord, Paul asked Timothy to come to him as soon as possible,
Demas had forsaken him, Crescens went to Galatia and
Titus to Dalmatia. Only Luke is with Paul. Paul wants Timothy to
bring Mark when he comes, and to bring his coat from Troas, also
his books and parchments. Paul has sent Tychicus to Ephesus.

Lord, Paul warned Timothy about Alexander the coppersmith because he
bitterly contested what Paul was teaching. Then Paul prays, "Lord,
repay him for the evil he has done."

Lord, Paul said, there was no one with him when he made his first defense
before the judge. He prayed for those who deserted him, "May they
not be judged for what they did." Paul testified the Lord Jesus stood
by me, and gave me power so that the message of grace was
proclaimed for all the unsaved to hear it." On that occasion You
delivered him from being thrown to the lions. Paul stated, "The Lord
will always deliver us from danger, until it's time to go to Heaven."
Paul glorifies You for his deliverance thus far.

Lord, Paul told Timothy to greet Prisca and Aquila and the household of
Onesiphorus. Erastus is in Corinth, and he left Trophimus sick in
Miletus. He sends greetings from Eubulus, Pudens, Linus, Claudia
and the brethren. Paul wants Timothy to come before winter. Then
he prays, "May the Lord Jesus Christ be with you, and may you have
His grace."

Amen.

# Titus

## THE STORY OF WRITING
## THE BOOK OF TITUS

Date: A.D. 65 ∼ Written from: Northern Greece ∼ Written by: Paul

It has been a few months since I was released from my imprisonment in Rome. My time in prison was not physically restrictive. Rome allowed me to rent a second floor apartment so I could be with my friends—Luke, Timothy, and the others.

But no one showed up at my trial, so I was released. I had been imprisoned for four years and some thought it was wasted years, but they're wrong. It was then when I wrote the prison epistles to Ephesus, Philippi, and Colosse. I was able to win to Christ many Roman soldiers, some were transferred to Caesar's palace and others were sent around the world. They were employed by Rome but they were soldiers of Christ. They carried out the Great Commission given by Jesus Christ, carrying the Gospel to the ends of the earth.

It felt good to leave Rome and not have a Roman soldier constantly with me. But I still have scars on my wrist from the chains. Physical freedom felt almost as good as freedom in Christ from the law.

When I left Rome I visited Ephesus, then several places throughout Turkey. I visited the Island of Crete and planted some new churches there, to join the older churches already on the island. Because Titus was from Crete, I left him there to strengthen all the churches.

I trust Titus will have an excellent ministry in Crete. He's been with me since the Jerusalem Conference when we settled the controversy about circumcising Gentiles. Remember, Titus is a Gentile believer in Christ who has never been circumcised.

I wrote to Titus from the West Coast of Greece after I got word that Titus was having difficulty with the churches of Crete. Some of the older

Christians from the synagogues felt they knew more about organizing a church than Titus. I heard that some elders were using Jewish fables in their sermons, others were resorting to legalism, and still others were disputing over genealogies.[1]

When I heard of the problems, I immediately sat down to write a letter to Titus, my faithful associate. I had great faith in Titus but I did not trust the elders of the churches. Titus was a young man capable of tough tasks; I once sent him to settle problems in Corinth because I knew he was dependable and diligent.[2] Even though Titus had strength of character, he also had great tact and love.[3]

I had led Titus to Christ and I will write to him about our common faith.

The churches in Crete are struggling with false teaching and they are resisting the leadership of Titus; so I decided to write to Titus noting, "For this cause I left you in Crete, so you could set in order the things that are lacking in the churches and ordain elders in every church."

Then I thought, *"When this letter is copied and sent to all of the churches in Crete, they will allow Titus to organize the churches, appoint elders, and teach them the truth of the Gospel of Jesus Christ."*

Again I thought what I should include in the letter, and then I remembered the words that I had written to the Corinthians, "Titus is my partner and fellow worker."[4] This is the emphasis that I want the Christians in Crete to know. I want them to follow Titus, as they would follow me.

Sincerely yours in Christ,<br>
The apostle Paul

## Endnotes

1. Titus 1:10; 14; 3:9-10.

2. 2 Cor. 8:17; 2 Cor. 7:6; 2 Cor. 8:17.

3. 2 Cor. 7:13-15.

4. 2 Cor. 8:23.

# PRAYING THE BOOK OF TITUS

## Qualifications for Pastors

### Titus 1:1-16

Lord, Paul wrote to Titus, calling himself Your slave
> And a messenger of Jesus Christ.
Paul was commissioned to preach to the elect
> So they would have faith in the Word of God,
> And be transformed in this life and gain eternal life.
You cannot lie, You promised eternal life
> Before the world was created.
In Your plan, You revealed the Gospel to Paul,
> So he could share it with everyone.
Paul wrote to Titus who shared his ministry,
> Because Paul led Titus to Christ.
Paul prayed for Titus to experience grace and peace
> From You, the Father, and Christ Jesus, the Savior.

Lord, Paul left Titus in Crete to organize churches
> And appoint pastors in every town.
A pastor must have unquestioned character
> And be the husband of one wife.
His children must be believers
> And he must not be charged with disorderly conduct.
A pastor will be Your representative to the people;
> A pastor must be blameless, never arrogant,
> Short-tempered, violent, greedy, or a brawler.
A pastor must be hospitable, friendly,
> Self-disciplined, fair-minded, and dedicated.

He must have a firm grip on the message of salvation,
>    And must agree with the doctrine Paul taught,
So that he can teach sound doctrine to all,
>    And refute those who oppose it.

Paul said there were many rebellious Christians in Crete who must be
>    dealt with because they say all Christians must keep the Jewish
>    ceremonial Law. Paul told Titus to silence them because they
>    were ruining whole families just to make money. Then Paul
>    quoted a Cretian poet who said, "Cretians are nothing but liars,
>    dangerous beasts who live to fill their bellies." Therefore, Paul
>    wanted Titus to correct them harshly and point them to sound
>    doctrine, so they will stop doing what the legalists tell them to do.

Lord, those who are committed to purity
>    Will find purity in their search for truth.
Those who are rebellious and evil thinking
>    Will find the corruption they seek.
They claim to know God personally,
>    But their actions deny their search for truth.
They are outrageously rebellious toward You,
>    And everything they do is evil.
>    Amen.

## The Work of a Pastor

### Titus 2:1-15

Lord, Paul told Titus to teach sound doctrine,
>    Tell the older men to be serious about the truth,
Self-disciplined, dignified, and do everything patiently and quietly;
>    But most of all, they must be men of faith.

Lord, Paul told Titus to teach the older women
>    That they must be holy in behavior,

And that they must not gossip nor get drunk,
And be the teachers of godliness.
Older women must teach the younger women,
To behave rightly, love their husbands,
And love their children.
Younger women must be sexually pure, gentle,
Keep their houses clean and obey their husbands
So they don't disgrace the Gospel with their lifestyle.

Lord, Paul told the younger men to behave,
And be serious about their duties in life.
They should be an example of sincerity and honesty,
And keep their promises,
So no one can accuse them of lying,
And they must not take advantage of others financially.

Lord, Paul told the workers to be obedient to their bosses,
And obey the orders given to them,
And never steal anything from them
But be completely honest at all times.
Slaves must strive to be an example of Christianity
In everything they do.

Lord, You revealed Your grace to us,
And made it available to the entire human race.
You have taught us to deny ourselves of everything
That does not lead us to godliness.
You have taught us to deny our pride and sinful ambitions,
To discipline ourselves, and live good lives,
Here and now in this present world.

Lord, I am looking for the blessed hope and glorious appearing
Of Jesus Christ my Savior and God.
He sacrificed Himself for me
To set me free from all contamination and wickedness.

Jesus has purified His people to be His very own,
      And He always wants them to do the right thing.
Paul told Titus to teach these truths
      Then rebuke any who would not listen to him,
      And finally don't let anyone despise him personally.
                Amen.

## Command to Godly Living

### Titus 3:1-15

Lord, I will be obedient to government officials,
      And will obey all civic laws,
      And I'll work honestly for a living.
I will not slander government rulers,
      Nor will I pick fights with them.
But I will be courteous to them
      And be kind to all people.
I remember I was once foolish
      And rebellious to laws, and rude to people
      Because I was a slave to my lust.
I lived for sinful pleasures, hating people,
      And being hated by them.

Lord, then You revealed Your kindness and love to save me;
      I was not saved by my works of righteousness,
      But was saved by your mercy.
You washed my sins way, and I was born again
      By the working of the Holy Spirit in my life
Which you abundantly poured out to me
      Through Jesus Christ my Savior.
Jesus did this so I might be justified in Your sight,
      And became Your heir,
        Looking forward to inheriting eternal life with You.

Lord, this is Your truth that I rely on,
     And will affirm it constantly,
That they who believe in You for salvation
     Must be careful to maintain good works.
This truth is good and it works for me,
     And will work for all who believe it.

Lord, Paul told Titus not to argue over pointless questions,
     And genealogies, and controversies over the Jewish Law.
     They are useless and cannot help anyone.
If anyone quarrels about this truth after the first and second rebuke,
     Put him out of the Church.
That type of person has already condemned himself,
     And has rejected the truth.

Lord, Paul promised to send Artemas or Tychicus to Titus, and then he was to join him at Nicopolis when Paul decided to spend the winter. He told Titus to make travel plans for Zenas the lawyer and Apollos. Paul wanted all believers to help others who have need, this makes their lives productive. Everyone with Paul sent greetings to Titus, and he finally prays, "Grace be with you."
     Amen.

# Philemon

## THE STORY OF WRITING THE BOOK OF PHILEMON

Date: A.D. 64 ❧ Written from: Rome, Italy ❧ Written by: Paul

When I came to Rome as a prisoner, I was scheduled to be sequestered in the Mamertine prison. All the cells are below ground—dark and dreary. But because I'm a political prisoner, I was allowed to rent a room if I had the money. But of course I had to pay all expenses, including the cost of Roman soldiers to guard me 24 hours a day. But God was merciful to me, I rented a second floor apartment with a balcony overlooking the street and the agora (marketplace).

The early morning sun poured between the tall buildings on either side of the street onto my balcony, making it a wonderful place for prayer and relaxation. When I go there to pray, no one disturbs me. The Roman guard—one of four stationed in the apartment 24 hours a day—gave me freedom. He knew I would not jump from the balcony, nor would I try to escape.

Everyone in the apartment heard the rattle of chains when I lifted my hands to pray. It reminded them that even though I was free in Christ, I was a prisoner of Rome. I had been sent to Rome to be tried by Caesar. But when my name was added to the docket of Caesar, I was told it would be two years until my hearing before Caesar.

My apartment was paid for by a rich Christian who pastored a church way up in the mountains. This church leader—Theophilus—had given Luke ten thousand pieces of silver to pay for my needs and the needs of my friends in Rome. But Theophilus was a crafty businessman, in return for the ten thousand pieces of silver, he asked Luke to write an accurate account of the growth of the early church—the Acts of the Apostles. While I was praying on the balcony, Luke was sequestered in a small room, writing the history of Christianity. Each morning Luke interviewed individuals to get the history of the early church, and in the afternoons, he wrote what he learned.

Just as Luke had previously written the life of Christ from his careful research all over the Holy Land, so he wrote the Acts of the Apostles following the same model. He had gathered notes from everyone he interviewed over the years. Just as the Holy Spirit had guided Luke *anothen* (from above) to guarantee the accuracy of the gospel of Luke, so the Holy Spirit was guaranteeing the words of Acts.

One morning I was praying for the little church in Colosse of Turkey, a small village not too far from the capital city of Turkey, Ephesus. I prayed for each person in the church, then I prayed for the slaves in the villa where the church met.

Then a providential thing happened. As I looked on the street, I suddenly saw a face that reminded me of one of the servants in Colosse for whom I just prayed. I cupped my hands to yell out over the balcony railing, **"Hey,…Onesimus,…up here…look this way…I remember you."**

Onesimus was shocked that someone in the city of Rome knew him by name. He had been a slave in the villa of Philemon. Later I learned Onesimus was an escaped slave.

Onesimus had known where his master's money was kept. He worked in the house, as opposed to a field slave. Onesimus waited for his opportunity. It came when he learned of a ship leaving on a certain night from Ephesus to Rome. This was Onesimus' lifetime opportunity for freedom. He had his escape plotted out. He stole the money, ran through the back wood paths over the hills to Ephesus, so no one would see him on the main road. He boarded the ship right before it sailed, paid for his ticket, and by the time Philemon missed him, Onesimus was gone from Turkey.

Now…here in Rome…a familiar voice called his name. Onesimus looked up to recognize me calling to him from the balcony. He realized, *"That's the preacher who came to my master's house to tell us the Gospel."* Onesimus thought, *"this preacher will turn me over to the Roman soldiers."*

I yelled down from the balcony, "**Wait**...I am sending Timothy down to get you. We want you to have lunch with us."

Onesimus first looked down the street one way, then the other way. A soldier was standing at both corners. He thought, *"If Paul yells out, the soldiers will arrest me."*

So Onesimus yelled back up to me to say he would enjoy having lunch with me and the other followers of Jesus Christ.

At the lunch table, it was then I found out that Onesimus had run away, and stolen money. I knew immediately that if Onesimus was turned over to the soldiers, they may imprison him or even kill him. Even if Onesimus were returned to Colosse and Philemon, his master had the right to execute Onesimus. If not death, surely Philemon would punish him severely.

I presented the Gospel to Onesimus, preaching to one man as passionately as I had preached on Mars Hill, or before many Jewish synagogues. As Onesimus listened carefully, he became convicted of his sin and was sorry for his crime. But there was another feeling; Onesimus felt the love of God flowing to him. Suddenly, in the middle of our conversation Onesimus had a great desire to know Jesus Christ intimately as Savior. When I bowed my head and led him in prayer, Onesimus offered the sinner's prayer,

"Lord Jesus, come into my heart and save me for I am great sinner..."

For the next six months Onesimus slept on a cot near the back door. He was happier than he had ever been in is life, for he was serving the Lord by doing what he was trained to do. Onesimus was serving me as a house servant. He immediately began keeping the apartment clean, sweeping the floors each day, and preparing meals.

After six months, I planned to send Tychicus to Turkey to carry a letter to the church at Ephesus and Colosse. These letters would circulate to other churches explaining the riches they had in Christ Jesus.

Then one morning I announced, "Onesimus...I am sending you with Tychicus back to Philemon...."

All of the believers with me looked from one set of eyes to the other. They were not sure this was the wise thing to do. Yes, they appreciated the house work done by Onesimus, but they were more concerned about his safety if he went back to Philemon.

Onesimus also had the greatest concern. He dropped his eyes to the floor and wouldn't look anyone. Even though there was no eye contact, the men in the room could see terror in Onesimus' facial expression.

"Don't worry," I said, "God will go with Onesimus as he returns home to Colosse." Then I explained, "This is the right thing to do, Onesimus must go back to rectify the situation."

I told the men, "I have prayed about this and I plan to write a letter to Philemon telling him how he should deal with this issue. I believe God will hear my prayer and Philemon will receive our brother Onesimus back with open arms."

I told the men sitting around the table that Philemon would do what I asked because I had led Philemon to faith in Christ, just as I had done for Onesimus. "I will write to praise Philemon for all of his love and faith in following Jesus Christ, I will give him our appreciation for the financial gift that he had sent."

Then I explained that I would write of my affection for Onesimus and how he had done the house work for us in Rome. I said to them, "I will ask Philemon to receive him back, not as a slave, but as 'beloved brother.' I am so sure that Philemon will take him back," I assured my followers, "I will offer to pay any expenses that Onesimus has incurred."

Then I laughed and said, "I will tell Philemon that I am coming to visit Colosse and that he should prepare my favorite room."

Everyone around the table laughed and agreed that the letter should be sent in the hands of Onesimus and Tychicus, and that Philemon would do the right thing.

Sincerely yours in Christ,<br>
The apostle Paul

# PRAYING THE BOOK OF PHILEMON

## A Prayer for Forgiveness and Restoration

### Philemon 1–25

Lord, Paul wrote a letter with Timothy from his prison in Rome to Philemon,
a rich Christian in Colosse. The letter was also addressed to
Philemon's wife Apphia, and to his son Archippus, a church leader
in the Colossian church.

*Lord, I pray for grace and peace in my life*
*The same as Paul prayed for Philemon's life.*
*Give me that grace and peace*
*From You, my heavenly Father and the Lord Jesus Christ.*

Lord, Paul thanked You for Philemon
And continued praying for him.
That Philemon would keep trusting the Lord Jesus
And develop deep love for Your children.

*Lord, I thank You for men like Philemon*
*Who have influenced my life of service for You.*
*Thank You that they enriched my life.*

Lord, Paul said Philemon had fully committed
Himself to the work of God,
And as Philemon put his generosity to work,
He would understand what he could really accomplish;
Philemon's generosity had given Paul joy and comfort,
And refreshed Paul's heart in serving God.

*Lord, may I use my resource generously in Your service*
*To bless and minister to others.*

Lord, Paul boldly asked a favor from Philemon,
  Even though Paul could have demanded it
  Because of all he had done for Philemon.
Paul asked that his request be received from a friend,
  Now an old man in prison for the sake of Christ.

Lord, Paul requested kindness be shown to Onesimus,
  A runaway slave from Philemon,
  That Paul had led to Christ;
Onesimus was not much use to Philemon in the past,
  But now Onesimus is useful to both of them
  Because he had been serving Paul in prison.

Paul says, I am sending Onesimus back to you
  And part of my heart comes back with him.

*Lord, just as the name Onesimus means useful,*
  *May I be useful to You and to others.*

Lord, Paul really wanted to keep Onesimus in Rome
  To do things for him that he couldn't do,
  Because his chains restricted him.
Onesimus could have helped Paul's ministry
  And that would be Philemon's contribution to Paul,
But Paul didn't want to make Onesimus stay in Rome
  Without Philemon's consent;
And Paul didn't want to force Philemon
  To let Onesimus stay in Rome with him.

Lord, Onesimus ran away for a little while,
  So Philemon could have him permanently.
But not taken back just as a slave,
  But received as a beloved brother in Christ.

Onesimus will do more for Philemon now as a brother
      Than he previously did as a slave because
      Now he belongs to You.

Lord, Paul asked Philemon to receive Onesimus
      As he would receive Paul.
If Onesimus has stolen anything
      Or cost Philemon any money,
Paul says, "Put that on my account
      And I will repay it to you"
      (Paul won't mention Philemon owes him his very life).

Lord, this letter is a wonderful picture of Christianity;
      Just as Onesimus ran away from his master,
      So I was straying away from You.

Just as Paul promised to pray for Onesimus' damages,
      So Christ paid for all the damages
      That sin did to my relationship with You.
Just as Paul prays for Philemon to receive Onesimus,
      So Christ prays for You to receive me.

Lord, Paul trusted Philemon to respond positively,
      Then added Philemon would do more than he asked.
Lord, Paul added one more request, "Get a room ready,
      I'm praying God will send me to see you."
Paul sent greetings from Epaphras, Mark,
      Aristarchus, Demas, and Luke, his co-laborers.

*Lord, as Paul prayed for the grace of the Lord Jesus Christ*
      *To be on his friend, Philemon,*
      *I pray for the same grace in my life.*
                 Amen.

# PERSONAL MESSAGE FROM GOD

_____

_____

_____

_____

_____

_____

_____

_____

_____

_____

_____

# ABOUT THE AUTHOR

Dr. Elmer Towns is an author of popular and scholarly works, a seminar lecturer, and dedicated worker in Sunday school. He has written over 125 books, including several best sellers. In 1995 he won the coveted Gold Medallion Book Award for *The Names of the Holy Spirit*.

Dr. Towns co-founded Liberty University with Jerry Falwell in 1971 and now serves as Dean of the B.R. Lakin School of Religion and as professor of Theology and New Testament.

Liberty University was founded in 1971 and is the fastest growing Christian university in America. Located in Lynchburg, Virginia, Liberty University is a private, coeducational, undergraduate and graduate institution offering 38 undergraduate and 15 graduate programs serving over 25,000 resident and external students (9,600 on campus). Individuals from all 50 states and more than 70 nations comprise the diverse student body. While the faculty and students vary greatly, the common denominator and driving force of Liberty University since its conception is love for Jesus Christ and the desire to make Him known to the entire world.

**For more information about Liberty University, contact:**

**Liberty University**
**1971 University Boulevard**
**Lynchburg, VA 24502**
**Telephone: 434-582-2000**
**E-mail: www.Liberty.edu**